THE REALM

THE REALM

An Unfashionable Essay on the Conversion of England

Aidan Nichols O.P.

ST PAULS

ST PAULS Publishing
187 Battersea Bridge Road, London, SW11 3AS, UK
www.stpaulpublishing.com

Cover picture: *The Wilton Diptych*
© National Gallery, London

ISBN 978-085439-800-3

Printed and bound in Great Britain by Intype Libra Ltd
Wimbledon, London, UK

ST PAULS is an activity of the priests and brothers of the Society of St Paul who proclaim the Gospel through the media of social communication.

What we can do is to use our minds, remembering that a tradition without intelligence is not worth having, to discover what is the best life for us not as a political abstraction, but as a particular people in a particular place, what in the past is worth preserving and what should be rejected, and what conditions, within our power to bring about, would foster the society that we desire.

T. S. Eliot, *After Strange Gods*

Nor indeed is even the 'Catholic' element there because I happen to be a Catholic, but rather because historically speaking (and leaving aside the truth or untruth of the Christian religion) it is the Catholic thing which has determined so much of our history and conditioned the thought of us *all.*

David Jones, *Dai Greatcoat*

Contents

Acknowledgements

The author is grateful to the editor of *The Catholic Herald* for permission to use an earlier version of Chapter 1 originally published in that paper on 23 July 1999; to the respective editors for permission to cite in Chapter 2 some material originally published in the United States in *Anglican Embers. Quarterly Journal of the Anglican Use Society* I. 7 (2005), pp. 171-195, and in the United Kingdom in *New Blackfriars* 87. 1010 (2006), pp. 337-356; and to the editor of *Josephinum* for permission to use an earlier version of Chapter 5, originally published in *Josephinum* 13. 1 (2006), pp. 66-80.

Preface

Issuing from a Catholic publishing house, the sub-title of this book, I suppose, makes the meaning of its title relatively plain. As a Catholic Christian and a patriotic Englishman (and, within that context, Briton), I wish my countrymen/women to share the blessings I have received. What could be more (super)natural? However, this book is not on theological doctrine, so I cannot be as eloquent as I might like about what those 'blessings' might be. For that, interested readers could look elsewhere in what I have written, for instance a short book from the year 2000, *Come to the Father*, the sub-title of which is 'An Invitation to Share the Catholic Faith'.[1]

En route to describing the goal of England's conversion, I have something to say in these pages about culture and civilisation, history and literature, ethics and philosophy, and even politics and economics. That is necessary if Catholic Christianity is to be proposed not as an occupation for individuals in their solitude but as a form for the public life of society in its overall integrity.

Of course most people will disagree with my aim, never mind my methods. That is why this is 'an unfashionable essay'.

Blackfriars
Cambridge
Feast of the Archangels, 2007

[1] *Come to the Father. An Invitation to Share the Catholic Faith* (London 2000).

Chapter 1

The Conversion of England

Introduction

The phrase 'the conversion of England', is one we have heard little of in recent years for reasons connected with the specifically contemporary-Catholic form of political correctness. It is a phrase of which I would like us to hear more. I shall not, then, be apologising for the phrase 'the conversion of England' in the way Cardinal Basil Hume was made to do after a famous interview with the editor of *The Tablet* newspaper for his 70th birthday – though admittedly to invoke the idea in the immediate circumstances of the crisis caused to the Church of England by the General Synod's vote for the ordination of women priests was not a high point of ecclesiastical diplomacy.[2]

Why 'England'?

Why single out 'England' for special mention at all? Should not 'England' content itself with being a portion, simply, of the North Atlantic archipelago?[3] And what is implied in such Anglocentrism for the

[2] This incident has been written up in A. Howard, *Basil Hume: the Monk Cardinal* (London 2005), pp. 222-223.

[3] As in N. Douglas, *The Isles. A History* (London 1999). But the bulk of the population of the English counties recognises itself as English, while the chief thread that unifies the historical story of this island is the English nation-state which came to include Wales (by conquest) and Scotland (by dynastic and subsequently parliamentary union).

Welsh, the Scots and the Irish? I have no message specifically for the Welsh, though it would not be hard to work out for Welsh Catholicism a vision analogous to the one I shall propose for English. (I will also be drawing on an Anglo-Welsh 'sage', David Jones, thus showing that my account acknowledges the debt of the Anglo-Saxons to the Romanised Britons, among whom the Welsh take pride of place.) The Scots, by contrast, play a part in my scheme chiefly because of the new flourishing of their common identity, signalled most dramatically in the opening of the new Parliament in Edinburgh and the resumption by the monarch of the title 'Queen of Scots', abandoned since 1707, on that occasion. I should argue, as Alex Salmond has done, that the confirmation of Scotland's distinct identity and destiny is something positive for England, for it is an opportunity for the English to take stock of their own distinctive life. I say this without seeking to foreclose (or even raise) the issue whether Scotland would be wise to recover its independence.

As to the Irish, they will enter my plot only obliquely, and not as the present-day citizens of the Irish Republic or indeed inhabitants of the island of Ireland as a whole but through the unavoidable historic fact that is Irish immigration – the immigration of the Irish into England from the end of the eighteenth century onwards, a movement of population continuing until so recently that writing in 1987 Michael Hornsby-Smith, the principal sociologist of English Catholicism, could estimate that within a total Catholic population in England of 4.2 million, 672,000 Catholics on English soil were Irish-born, and another 640,000, though born here, were the children of Irish parents: figures which amount together to between a quarter and a third of the total. Once again, I shall suggest that, seen aright, this can be regarded not as a negative but as a positive phenomenon for the conversion of the English people.

English Catholicism's decline

In *The Daily Telegraph* for 26 June 1999, the Catholic journalist Daniel Johnson wrote of the then recently deceased Basil Hume:

> Great spiritual leader that he was, Cardinal Hume leaves the Catholic Church in this country in a parlous state. It is now afflicted by dissension, apathy, too few vocations and an ageing congregation – the very malaises of the Church of England and the Nonconformists a generation earlier.

Assuming the broad correctness of this judgment (but 'parlous' is surely too strong), how has this state of affairs come about? One clue may be given in the survey by Hornsby-Smith, who concluded that by the 1980s Roman Catholicism in England had become what he termed a 'domesticated denomination', unlikely to rock any boats in culture or society.[4] He spoke of an 'erosion of the distinctiveness of English Catholicism' whereby the community seemed set to become

> cosily absorbed and dissolved … in an increasingly secular society, indistinguishable in its religious beliefs

[4] M. Hornsby-Smith, *Roman Catholics in England. Studies in Social Structure since the Second World War* (London 1987), p. 216.

> and values from other Christian bodies and in its social and political morality from other citizens. [5]

Actually, the impression Hornsby-Smith gives is that, personally, he would not particularly regret it if Catholicism in England *did* become doctrinally indistinguishable from other varieties of Christianity. But he *would* regret it if it failed to be, in his words, 'prophetic' and 'challenging', vis-à-vis secular society by means of an 'option for the poor' – in, presumably, a national or, in the buzz-word, 'inculturated', version of Latin American liberation theology. Just so he would also regret it if there were no forthcoming new Ecumenical Council to, as he explains, sweep away priestly celibacy, license contraception, permit the remarriage of the divorced and the ordination of women, all in the context of re-establishing Christian unity.

That also seems to be the hope which animated Vicky Cosstick, formerly director of pastoral formation in the Archbishop of Westminster's seminary, Allen Hall. Writing in the monthly magazine *Priests and People* (now *The Pastoral Review*), she remarked that, failing that outcome – or, at the very least, a new strategically planned regime of mixed priestly-lay governance in parishes – the Catholic Church in England will limp further into institutional decline:

> Parishes will close, and a patchwork of remedies will emerge, depending on the approach of different dioceses: parishes run by priests of low calibre, inadequately formed and supported; parishes run by

[5] Ibid., p. 42.

> parish pastoral councils and lay pastoral administrators; some run by 'reverse missionaries' from the Third World; some by deacons, ex-Anglicans, groups of Religious sisters. The diversity amongst parishes will increase. In this scenario, faith and spirituality continue to become increasingly privatised and individualised, with odd pockets of reactionary and right-wing, sectarian and barely Christian devotion.[6]

It is, I suppose, possible that what unites these writers is a desire, like that of the Fat Boy in Dickens, to make our flesh creep, our blood run cold and our hair stand on end, just for the fun of it. But hard figures reach us in a 'special report' entitled catchily 'Where Have all the Catholics Gone?', to be found in the issue of *The Tablet* for 19 June 1999. This report reproduces, simply, an analysis of figures indicative of the present state of health or otherwise of the Catholic Church in England, an analysis carried out by the managing director of 'Opinion Research Business' (and formerly of the far better known Gallup Poll.)[7] It had already been claimed by the most recent edition of the *United Kingdom Christian Handbook* (sub-title *Religious Trends 1985-1990*) that in those five years at the end of the 1980s, Catholics suffered the highest rate of numerical decline of any religious group in the United Kingdom. The new survey reproduced in *The Tablet* considered a broader slice of time, from 1964 to 1997. The number of Baptisms had more than halved since 1964, and taken

[6] V. Cosstick, 'Adapt or Die', *Priests and People* 13. 6 (1999), p. 225.
[7] G. Heald, 'Where have all the Catholics gone?', *The Tablet*, 19 June 1999, pp. 860-863.

in tandem with the increase in the nominally Catholic population suggested that roughly half of Catholic parents no longer baptise their children in a Catholic church – a statistic which if true would lead of course to further and accelerated decline. Confirmations had fallen by almost 50 per cent from their peak in 1964. There had been in the period studied a decline of over a quarter in the number of priests, the total of whom by 1997 was lower than thirty years ago when the Catholic population was well under two-thirds of what it is presently, though since the beginning of the 90s the number of ordinations had slightly increased. Only a third of the number of marriages celebrated in Catholic churches in 1964 were registered in 1997. From 1974 to 1997 the number of conversions had remained stable at just over 5000 yearly, well under half the tally midway through the Second Vatican Council. But here Opinion Research Business's manager commented that, at the end of the period, had there been no incoming Anglicans sent swimming across the Tiber by the decision of the General Synod to ordain women, the Catholic Church would not be able to record any statistically significant number of converts at all. Finally, in the tale of woe, Mass attendance had dropped by almost half since 1964, so that by the end of the 90s just over a quarter of Catholics appear to attend Mass weekly.

In the last two or three years, these figures have been considerably ameliorated in the south-east of the country, and in some major cities elsewhere, thanks to new immigration, chiefly from Eastern Europe. It remains to be seen how many of these new economic migrants will seek to remain, as distinct from 'make a packet' and return. And in any case, the likely pace of economic development of the former Communist societies west of Russia is such that repeated waves of Slavonic immigration, lasting as long as their Irish predecessors, should not be anticipated.

No doubt a lot could be said by way of commentary on and interpretation of these statistics. Compared with some other Western European countries, a figure of 25 per cent of Catholics practising regularly might be thought highly respectable. But though lapsation has always been a phenomenon of post-Reformation Catholicism in England, that figure does not compare favourably with any plausible estimates for the period since the nineteenth-century Catholic Revival began.[8]

What is the cause?

Let me begin by simply stating my conviction that, contrary to the gloss put on these figures by *The Tablet* in the editorial which prefaced the issue where the Opinion Research analysis appeared, the key to the situation is not dissent. The key is apathy. The reason for the decline is not principled opposition to the norms of Church doctrine and discipline though this may play a subsidiary part. Instead, it lies in an apathetic attitude towards the entire realm of religion, that cosmic framework within which the lives of the great majority of this country's inhabitants were once lived.

---

[8] For that heroic story of rebirth, see above all E. Norman, *The English Catholic Church in the Nineteenth Century* (Oxford 1984).

I find it incredible that if, at some Third Vatican Council, a progressive pope by the wave of a wand introduced into the Catholic Church that package of liberal reforms outlined by Mrs Cosstick and Dr Hornsby-Smith the effect of this would be to re-galvanise English Catholicism which would at once begin to recover its lapsed in large numbers and re-vitalise its parishes. The justification for such incredulity on my part is that all the desiderata such critics set forward are now already achieved in the Church of England. Bearing in mind that Anglicanism's decline in England has been only slightly less rapid than that of the Catholic Church, we can ask rhetorically, To what apostolic effect has this been? The minuscule proportions of the effect suggest that apathy about the religious dimension is a far more plausible motor of decline than is dissent. I am sorry to speak sharply about the authors mentioned. But it is hard to avoid the impression that the nerve of such writing is a dislike of traditional Catholicism as such. Within limits, pastoral flexibility is a good thing. But we need to recover confidence in the Catholic tradition, as corporately interpreted by the magisterium of the Church. And not to disparage our 'product': that is a requirement of any sane marketing strategy.[9]

[9] Mgr Keith Barltrop, the first head of the newly formed agency for evangelisation of the Catholic Church in England and Wales has written, in evident exasperation: 'We've got to have confidence in who we are. I sometimes use a business analogy, which is anathema to a lot of clergy. Imagine that you were a business man who didn't believe in your product; when you went into the market-place you said: "What we've got to sell is only one thing among many, and it's got a lot of problems. And we're not really asking you to buy

Committed Catholics know that the religious dimension is not simply one dimension among others in life. Rather, that dimension gives access to the divine revelation which shows us the total content of truth, goodness and beauty in which our lives as a whole are set. Apathy about the religious dimension was bound to set in, however, if the desire to throw open more windows from the Church to the world coincided – as by a piece of really unfortunate timing in the 1960s it *did* coincide – with the increasing secularisation of that world. And it only made things worse that the Church herself compounded the problem by exacerbating certain weaknesses in her own self-presentation – doctrinally, philosophically, liturgically, artistically, socially, and so on.

If, as I think is true, a blurring of the image of what Catholic Christianity should be took place simultaneously with a loss of confidence in just how important it was to be connected to religion anyhow, it was only to be expected that the role of Catholicism among populations in countries undergoing secularisation would become more and more tenuous. And so, at least in England, it transpired.

But tears over spilled milk, as the proverb warns us, are wasted effort. Now it's happened, we have to think what to do about it. Both the Second Vatican Council and Pope John Paul II adjured Catholics to seek to read the 'signs of the times'. Those 'signs' are: any indicators in

---

it ..." That's actually what we do as Catholics a lot of the time. It's crazy': 'How to Evangelise', part 2, *The Catholic Herald*, 6 July 2007, p. 8.

general history as to how we might proceed in spreading the Gospel. One sign of the times for a renaissance of Catholic Christianity in England can be found, I think, in the debate going on over English identity – a debate largely sparked off by two things: events north of the Border and the coming of the European Union. Why I say this debate about England could be important for us is in one sense simple to explain, in another sense complex and many-sided.

The debate about England

Let me at this point confine myself to the simple but mention the complex. The simple reason is this. If it can be shown that Catholic Christianity was not only essential to the making of England but provides the best foundation – intellectual, moral and social – for the culture of an England re-made, then the outlines of what Catholicism is will by that very fact be clarified and its importance gauged at its true worth. This offers a strategy for the mobilisation of believers, for encouraging them to enter the debate about the wellsprings, roots and chief historical determinants of the English contribution to international humanity and the future orientation of an English culture and society, steadied by a fuller grasp of this historic patrimony. And here the aim should be not just to enter an ongoing debate.[10] For Catholic Christians

[10] See at a scholarly level, K. Kumar, *The Making of English National Identity* (Cambridge 2003), a sociological approach, or E. Jones, *The English Nation. The Great Myth* (Stroud [1998] 2003), an historical one; or at a more popular level, J. Paxman, *The English. A Portrait of a People* (Harmondsworth 1999, 2nd edition), R. Scruton, *England. An Elegy* (London 2000).

the aim is really to communicate our faith to others as what made England once and can remake it again.

Of course there are many aspects to that claim which is where the complexity I mentioned comes in. Just to name a few examples. There is the issue of whence do we get the virtues that we hold in respect or need to rediscover in society. There is the issue of whether the civility of our political system (as distinct from its simply following the majority, which can get you anywhere as the example of Germany's Third Reich shows) depends on assumptions about humane behaviour drawn ultimately from the Judaeo-Christian revelation.[11] There is the issue of the degree to which the idea of 'the Crown' can be separated off from the idea of Christian monarchy. Many of the metropolitan elite today are republicans,[12] but presumably they are civilised republicans, and so there is the question too of the indebtedness of the founders of our literary tradition

---

[11] In his war-time *Lettre aux Anglais*, Georges Bernanos apostrophised the American president: 'I've had enough, dear Mr Roosevelt, of hearing about the democracies being opposed to the dictatorships, even by M. Maritain. Democracy furnishes no defence whatever against dictatorships, and that's the truth'. Cited B. E. Doering, *Jacques Maritain and the French Catholic Intellectuals* (Notre Dame, Indiana, and London, 1983), pp. 186-187.

[12] Assuming they are also adherents of the European Union the following comment may be pertinent. Neil MacCormick, a constitutional lawyer, in his *Questioning Sovereignty. Law, State and Nation in the European Commonwealth* (Oxford 1999), is a convinced Europhile but agrees that the EU is perceived as a faceless 'oligo-bureaucratic' body. He regrets the absence of 'a single individual, elected or chosen by some reasonable process, who, in a significant sense, personifies or bears the overall persona of the Union' – in short the absence of a monarch in a role of unifying a society which only a monarch can do well. Prescient later mediaeval counsellors would have advised him to marry a Byzantine princess to a Habsburg.

– Chaucer, Shakespeare – to a Catholic metaphysic and ethic. (Peter Ackroyd's *Albion*, from which I take the name of my second chapter in this book, argues for the mediaeval – and especially the Anglo-Saxon – roots of the English imagination, rather than treating a distinctive English cultural identity as a creature of the Reformation.[13]) And again there is the question of how much the strengths shown by the English people in times of tribulation (during the London Blitz, for example) are owed to the continuation of a latent Christianity that, under the impact of stress, expressed itself in prayers and actions not entirely unrelated to the theological virtues of faith, hope and charity.

It is arguable that, in terms of its origins and the crucial formative phase of its development, England is in fact inseparable from Catholicism, unimaginable without it. In the pre-Conquest period, England was created by the joint efforts of the Church and an Anglo-Saxon kingship which itself attained to the consciousness of its people-forming role through the biblical and patristic models of kingship proposed by the Church. In the post-Conquest period the legal notions of common, civilian and ecclesiastical lawyers were influenced by the way natural law and equity appear in the light of revelation when framing standards for what was to count as fair and reasonable practice – something that underlies the English sense of the 'reasonable man' and 'fair play'. At the same time the emphasis given to virtues like mercy and justice in the rites of induction of the sovereign

[13] P. Ackroyd, *Albion. The Origins of the English Imagination* (London 2002).

is unthinkable without the Church's interpretation of biblical and classical ideas and norms. In the Renaissance period, which takes us up to the Tudors and so the end of the Catholic phase of English history, we can ask whether the English literary canon could have reached its maturity without the help of the Catholic theological concepts of nature and of good and evil implicit in, for example, Shakespeare's plays. And without wanting to descend too far into trivia, innumerable tiny indicators in English customary life confirm that 'Old Catholic England' remained present in occluded forms: from the adaptation of clerical robes in the dress of judges and academics, through gestures like Parliamentarians bowing to the Speaker (originally an obeisance to the altar of the Chapel of St Stephen in Westminster Palace) or members of the Royal Navy 'saluting the quarter-deck' (where the crucifix was hung on board ship in Catholic times), to sayings like 'touch wood' (a reference to touching the wood of relics of the True Cross), in the survival of place-names like the Greyfriars, Whitefriars and Blackfriars Streets found in many English towns, inn-signs of various descriptions and the popular names (often Marian) of wild flowers.[14]

Without wanting to take up a formally English-national position, I think we might agree that the phrase 'Catholic England' makes a lot of historical sense, whereas the phrase 'Catholic Britain' sounds somewhat paradoxical when we bear in mind how much the modern notion of Britain, which comes

[14] For numerous details, see M. Elvins, *Old Catholic England* (London 1978).

from the eighteenth century, replacing the earlier idea of the united realms of England and Scotland, owes to anti-Catholic propaganda. It was a way of uniting two Protestant kingdoms against the perceived threat of Catholic Europe for which read 'France'.[15]

Dialogue and mission

Those who support the politically correct ban on speaking about 'the conversion of England' which Cardinal Hume transgressed in the eyes of those who fear ruffling ecumenical and inter-faith feathers (and arousing the irritation of secularists) sometimes appeal to the example and documents of the Second Vatican Council. Surely the Council replaced the mission to convert non-Catholics by dialogue with them instead? Certainly it mandated courtesy, respect and the seeking of common ground in dialogue with separated Christians, adherents of other religions as well as humanists. But it did not understand such dialogue as meaning that mission must stop and putting into cold storage the universal claims of the Catholic Church.

Dialogue, I would suggest, is a means to mission and a condition for mission. It is a *means* to mission inasmuch as the exposure of the two parties in dialogue to the full range of each other's convictions offers an opportunity for the grace of God to convince the conscience of the other of Christian or Catholic truth – just as it also offers the possibility of suasion from that

[15] The thesis of L. Colley, *Britons: Forging the Nation 1707-1837* (London 1996).

truth. It is a *condition* of mission in that only a thorough grasp of the ideas and values of the other can enable the missionary to locate those aspects of divine revelation which speak most acutely to the other's need.

To make coherent sense of the Council's various demands we must say something like that, because in fact Vatican II uses very strong language to commend the mission to convert. As its decree on missionary activity, *Ad Gentes*, puts it: according to the divine plan

> the whole human race is to form one People of God, coalesce into the one Body of Christ, and be built up into one Temple of the Holy Spirit.[16]

And a little later in the same text we read:

> It is not enough for the Christian people to be present and organised in a given nation. Nor is it enough for them to carry out an apostolate of good example. They are organised and present for the purpose of announcing Christ to their non-Christian fellow citizens by word and deed, and by aiding them toward the full reception of Christ.[17]

Ignoring these imperatives on the ground that, in a pluralist society, to refer to them is 'in bad taste' has damaged the Church. Hiding our light under a bushel makes people wonder whether we really are committed to our faith as something uniquely precious and desirable. It also, one could argue, creates what the theologians call an 'obex', an 'obstacle', to the development in Catholics themselves of the graces of Baptism and Confirmation.

---

[16] *Ad Gentes*, 7.
[17] Ibid., 15.

Those sacraments were instituted not only or even mainly for our personal sanctification. Above all, they are given for the insertion of individuals into the common mission of the Church which continues that of the apostles who in turn continue that of Christ whose own mission is the prolongation of his eternal procession from the Father as the divine Son – sent into time to bring back to the Father a world estranged from him. We can't for our own spiritual good just treat conversion as off the agenda and leave the whole issue to Evangelicals. That great evangelist pope John Paul II drove that point home in his encyclical *Redemptoris missio.*

When in the summer of 1999 I wrote an article in *The Catholic Herald* along the lines of this chapter, it was picked up by the BBC's 'Sunday Programme', and this led to a short hostile interview. The interviewer pressed me on the question of offence to other churches and other faiths if Catholics 'go back' to talking about 'the conversion of England', though I'd said nothing in fact about targeting practising members of other churches or practising adherents of other religions. I was also asked how I could warrant imposing my religion on other people. Of course, it isn't a matter of imposing. It's a matter of appealing to the freedom of others. And I expressed the hope that they might wish to be taken seriously enough to be addressed by me on these topics (in suitable circumstances), because I would hope to be taken sufficiently seriously in my turn to be addressed by them. But if Catholics were successful, the interviewer went on, this would have the effect of eliminating other Christian and non-Christian religions: surely a Bad

Thing. I made the point that, if Catholic Christianity conveys in human form the divine revelation which is the greatest truth, goodness and beauty man can know, then all the elements of truth, goodness and beauty in the theory and practice of other forms of Christianity and indeed in other faith traditions would attain their crown in this context, would come to their intended fulfilment. It's because I believe this to be true that for instance I support the existence of the Eastern Catholic churches, and the scheme for an Anglican church-body united to Rome but not absorbed. And so far as other faiths are concerned, I applaud the Association for Hebrew Catholics which sought a distinctive jurisdiction with its own ritual calendar for Catholic Jews, and sympathise with attempts to show how certain aspects of Hindu philosophy and devotion could be regarded as a 'preparation for the Gospel'; more needs to be done to study Buddhism and Islam in this light though in the case of Islam the term 'preparation' would probably be out of place.

Realism or fantasy?

But how well fitted is the Catholic Church in England, the so-called 'English Catholic Church', to launch a new mission to the people of England, remobilising energies ecclesial and sacramental, and ultimately, then, gracious and salvific – saving gifts from God – in the context of the question, If the Church once 'made England', can she now remake this not at the moment terribly impressive culture, dominated, for much of the time by supermarkets and sport, and in its more serious mood caught between nostalgia for the old Britain and its empire and admonitions to make a compact with 'Europe' which now means not what it meant to Pope St Pius V or, indeed, Goethe but a cosmopolitan bureaucracy presiding over a single economic market?

Actually, despite the scary statistics, I think the Church here *is* quite well fitted to take up this mighty challenge. And I say this mainly because the Catholic Church in England is not really the 'English Catholic Church' at all. That is, it is not a Church of ethnically pure Englishmen and women but something of a dog's dinner (a pot-pourri would be a more polite way of putting it) which includes, yes, recusant families and converts from Anglicanism and other things, but also a large constituency of Irish people and those descended from them, Italians, Poles, and other southern and eastern European immigrants, incomers from the New Commonwealth, Filipinos, Vietnamese and a lot more besides. Now if the original Anglo-Saxon conversion of England is anything to go by, what you need for a successful movement of conversion which really 'takes' and acts to transform culture across a whole society is precisely a mixture of indigenous and exogenous elements. You need people who come from within and people who come from without.

If we ask about the development of Christianity in dark age England, who were its great figures?, we would have to answer, Wilfrid and Cuthbert and Chad, who were of pure Anglo-Saxon stock, but also Augustine, an Italian, Theodore of Tarsus, who was Greek, and Aidan, who was a *Scotus* or, more or less, an Irishman. It stands to reason, really. If the protagonists of mission come exclusively from *within* the culture, they won't be able to see it with sufficient objective distance to judge what its christening requires. If on the other hand they come exclusively from *outside* the culture, they won't have the inner sympathy for it and the depth or simplicity of identification with its members which is prerequisite for winning others.

I could give another reason for saying that the ethnic mix of English Catholicism is a missionary advantage: namely, that, thanks to successive modern waves or at least trickles of immigration, the inhabitants of England are now themselves even more of a mongrel breed than once they were. And that is true though of course more so in Bradford than in Barnstaple, in Notting Hill than in Norwich. Unlike some people, I don't believe this unevenly distributed multi-ethnicity means that to talk about 'English culture' is now a Very Bad Thing. How boring the world would be if an egalitarian multi-culturalism were forced to exist everywhere and Sikkim became indistinguishable except in its landscape from Sorrento or the Sahara, at least for those of us rich enough to be able to travel (and the tourist industry is now, I gather, the single largest employer in the world – and therefore of huge importance to the developing world as well as to lucky us).

The other cultures present in our country, Indian, Chinese or whatever, should be thought of not as displacements of the cultural mainstream but as potential enrichments of it. And *pace* the National Front or the

British National Party, what in any case should count is not our racial origin. What should count is our desire to have a common home. Immigrants to this country should come with a desire or willingness to enter its distinctive culture. At the absolute minimum, this will mean that they are happy to learn its language from which its culture is inseparable. They have, and it is right that they have, a *bipolar* existence. They do not, then, have a 'multicultural' one. The Catholic Church in England itself partakes of this bipolar existence by being a synthesis of immigrant and indigenous, and indeed one could argue that a typical Catholic church will always be like this, both wider than a given country and yet rooted in that country, at once internationalist as the Church of all nations, and yet patriotic, the soul of its society, because it is the Church of this place, our common home. By contrast we can say, the Church of England is too exclusively indigenous here to have much of that cutting edge that mission demands. The Orthodox Church, on the other hand, is too little indigenous here to have the ease of access that mission also demands. Both – cutting edge and ease of access – can be found, as it happens, in English Catholicism, though more by accident than by design. Catholicism can present itself as quintessentially English and generously inter-ethnic at one and the same time.

The need for a mission policy

I said that showing how Catholic Christianity played an essential role in the making of England must be backed up by showing the role it can play in the future remaking of England. What I like to call, using an admittedly old-fashioned word, 'Christendom' – by which I mean Catholic Christianity in its fullest possible manifestation in culture – must, like the Sleeping Beauty of legend, be kissed awake.

In a book called *Christendom Awake,* I tried to make a list of policies we need if as a Church we are to turn things around – not only reviving as a community, but attracting people to the faith and bringing about a sea-change in the general outlook in England.[18] The list of policies includes:

- a revival of doctrine in catechetics and preaching, necessary if we are to present revelation as the greatest truth ever known
- a re-enchanting of the Liturgy so that by language, gesture, image, music, it brings before us the transcendent beauty of the Kingdom of God
- a recovery of metaphysics for which Thomist Catholics, indebted to the patrimony of thought left behind by St Thomas Aquinas, should be especially fitted, so as to give people a really coherent and deep philosophy of the created order
- renewing Christian political thought, which, *pace* liberation theology, is not simply about favouring the poor but has a much wider task, showing how to combine order and spontaneity in a spacious civil life lived under God
- the revivification of the family through the re-uniting

[18] A. Nichols, O.P., *Christendom Awake. On Re-energizing the Church in Culture* (Edinburgh 1999).

wherever possible of home and work, domestic life and economic production

- the resacralising of art and architecture so that they begin to be once more what they have always been in traditional culture: echoes of the divine order beyond the world as well as of the meaning we make within it
- a great emphasis on monasticism which is *the* sign of the radicalness of the difference that divine revelation makes, and, where relevant, the recreation of a classical Religious life in Orders and communities that have to a greater degree or less become secularised in their manner of living
- a new and more powerful rhetoric in defence of the unborn, the crucified innocents in our midst
- recovering a Catholic reading of the Bible and especially of the Gospels, a reading of Scripture in the same Spirit as that in which it was written, rather than in the light of academic fashion, so that we will find in the Bible what dogma and the Liturgy speak of: the divine-human Christ who knew the two natures to be united in his person, the Son of God and Son of Man.

There is a distinctively Catholic approach to all of these, and they all enter the Catholic synthesis because it is natural to the faith to shape a civilisation and not just be something for our private lives.

> [I]n the Christian system, the culture acts as a prism to the *lumen de lumine*, the light of the world; and the effect is to break up the system so that each part

> may be assimilated by the various kinds of social endeavour.[19]

Something I omitted to deal with in *Christendom Awake* was church schools as an instrument for communicating a revivified Catholicism. In his inaugural lecture in the chair of education at Christ Church Canterbury, James Arthur, a critic of much in the current functioning of church schools, spoke of the need for inspirational leadership in such schools by practising and believing Christians who accept their Church's teachings and can lead their school in prayer; insist on the centrality of religion in the life of the school community and ensure the priority of religious education as well as worship on the timetable; can establish a school community where the processes of faith and moral development are integrated; and articulate the Christian educational vision of the school through their ability to expound the philosophy of Christian education, see all things in the light of faith, and are able to set the school tone accordingly by sensitivity to the demands of justice and charity.[20] By at least this token reference I would like to make good that rather serious omission now.

I am under no illusions as to the monumental character of the task this set of desiderata entails. It is an absolutely colossal agenda, some of whose features we

---

[19] H. Grisewood, *The Painted Kipper* (London 1970), p. 65.

[20] In his work Arthur has been much concerned with the erosion of distinctive religious identity in contemporary education even when religious authorities are formally responsible for the schools involved: *The Ebbing Tide. Policy and Principles of Catholic Education* (Leominster 1995), idem., *Faith and Secularisation in Religious Colleges and Universities* (London 2006).

must re-visit, under the heading 'integral evangelisation', before this essay ends.

A provisional conclusion

T. S. Eliot, a Catholic-minded Anglican wrote:

> A Church is to be judged by its intellectual fruits, by its influence on the sensibility of the most sensitive and on the intellect of the most intelligent, and it must be made real to the eye by monuments of artistic merit.[21]

I would say that a Church must be judged first and foremost by the fruits of holiness it produces. And yet Eliot is quite right that it must also make its impact on culture, and that as by priority. Pope John Paul II said somewhere that the faith without a culture to go with it is like a soul without a body to express it.

This must be a holistic culture worthy of the faith of Jesus Christ the Creator and Redeemer God incarnate. It can only be brought into being, so far as it depends on us so to do, by a coordinated strategy for recreating a full-blooded catholicity with the power to fascinate and draw individual people to itself and transform a culture in all its principal dimensions. That is what the 'mission to convert' and 'the conversion of England' mean to me.

[21] T. S. Eliot, 'Lancelot Andrewes', in *Essays Ancient and Modern* (London 1936), p. 13.

Chapter 2

Albion

Origins

As a people, we began in multi-culturalism, which is not to say that we should end there. The Insular culture of Dark Age Britain from which England emerged was in contact with a variety of relatively homogeneous cultural entities further afield. From these it sought to make a synthesis at home. That is the message of that wondrous book the Lindisfarne Gospels. Quite apart from the sheer beauty of its craftsmanship, the historic significance of the book consists in its synthetic power to integrate a number of cultural contributions – all in the service of the divine Word which inspired the creative generosity the book represents. That makes it a fitting icon of the genesis of a nation. As the student of Anglo-Saxon England, Michelle Brown, explains:

> [S]uch a fusion of diverse elements drawn from all areas of a multi-cultural society may have been intentional on the part of the makers. For modern scholars the temptation is to isolate those features redolent of a particular culture or region with which they are concerned, sadly often at the expense of a balanced consideration of the whole. The collision between the traditions of the early 'Celtic' (or perhaps more properly in this context 'Columban') and 'Roman' Churches which resulted in the famous synod held at St Hild's double monastery at Whitby in 664, at

> which St Wilfrid won the day in favour of Rome, has perhaps been seen as too much of a divide between the two camps, significant though it undoubtedly was. The rift (and the schism it threatened) was healed fairly quickly, if not easily, thanks largely to the reconciliation undertaken by such figures as St Cuthbert, Bishop Ecgbert and Abbot Adomnán of Iona. Nonetheless, there remains a tendency for much modern nationalism to be projected backwards into a period which was notable for its ability to merge elements from the Celtic, Germanic, Graeco-Roman, and Christian Orient cultures to give birth to a new order in Europe: the early Middle Ages.[22]

For the makers of the Lindisfarne Gospel-book, this was, so Brown explains, a cause for legitimate pride:

> The apostolic mission had reached the farthest ends of the known world ... where a Christian people carried the Word of God still further northwards while showing the old centre, the Mediterranean, that they were no provincial outpost, but the champions of a new order.

And so

> The text of the Lindisfarne Gospels explodes into a triumphant celebration of the best of all cultures, as its letters grow to occupy the whole page – literally the Word made flesh [possibly an allusion to the calfskin used in book production], or rather the Word made word.[23]

As she explains, '"Celtic" did not preclude "Roman", or

---

[22] M. B. Brown, *The Lindisfarne Gospels. Society, Spirituality and the Scribe* (London 2003), p. 8.
[23] Ibid.

vice versa, except in the mind of a few die-hard scholars, then as now'.[24] On Brown's authoritative view, the Lindisfarne Gospels represent a fusion of earlier Celtic – 'Hiberno-Saxon' – and notably Columban traditions with Italian stimuli arriving in England through the twin monasteries of Wearmouth and Jarrow. They do so, she writes, 'in the service of a recognisable agenda'. And if we ask what that agenda might be, she replies it is one of cultural fusion for the sake of the emergence of a Christian nation.

> In many respects, the Lindisfarne Gospels are the visual equivalent of [Bede's] *Historia Ecclesiastica*, in terms of presenting a fully integrated, inclusive image for an emergent state formed of disparate cultural groups.[25]

And to explain that in turn:

> The three communities – Lindisfarne, Jarrow and Monkwearmouth – should be seen as working together to establish a new identity for Northumbria, and thereby for England, one which acknowledged the components which had established its Christian culture and which was as implicitly romanising as that promoted by Wilfrid, and symbolised by the purple codex which was the focus of his cult at Ripon, but which was intrinsically orientated towards displaying cultural synthesis and reconciliation within the Christian ecumen, interlacing and co-celebrating the Celtic, British, Anglo-Saxon, Germanic, Roman,

[24] Ibid., p. 9.

[25] Ibid., p. 407. For Bede in our perspective, see G. Tugène, *L'Idée de la nation chez Bède le Vénérable* (Paris 2001); *L'image de la nation anglaise dans l'"Histoire ecclésiastique" de Bède le Vénérable* (Paris 2001).

> Coptic, Byzantine and Syro-Phoenician traditions. The apostolic mission had indeed reached and embraced the far ends of the earth. The material and literary culture of these extremities proclaims that they were no provincial outpost, but a vibrant part of that universal, eternal communion.[26]

That is how England – Albion – began. What came to be the key elements in its heritage? Three may be identified speedily. Apart of course from the Church, which is the (literally!) fontal institution at the origins of Anglo-Saxon society, they are: the law, the crown, the parliament. With the Church these are the predominant institutions in England's story. As we shall see, they belong together in a social covenant suitable to a baptised nation.

Law: from covenant to correctness

The historian of Anglo-Saxon England Patrick Wormald argued that promulgation of *lage* – 'laws' – by the Anglo-Saxon and Anglo-Danish kings had a wider role than merely communicating their legal content. As with the contemporary Carolingians in Continental Europe: '*lex* expressed royal *fidelitas* in return for that of the people'.[27] Henry I's major Charter of 1100 mirrors the Frankish practice by its issue at his coronation. In it, law – specifically the 'laga Eadwardi' – is something *promised*. 'Lex' is something *guaranteed*. In other words, reciprocity is integral to the ancient English understanding of law. In Magna Carta the giving of such guarantees about *lex*

[26] M. B. Brown, *The Lindisfarne Gospels*, op. cit., p. 408.

[27] P. Wormald, *The Making of English Law: King Alfred to the Twelfth Century. I. Legislation and its Limits* (Oxford 1999), p. 134.

is linked to undertakings not to remove anyone's *honor* without just judgment. In this regard, Magna Carta is not exceptional: suchlike promises often figured in mediaeval charters. This carries implications for a social covenant.

In the course of the thirteenth century, pressure would fall on common lawyers to make their law far more visible and intelligible in its articulation – this was almost certainly due to the competition they experienced from the Roman law which either in its pure form in civil jurisprudence or adapted in canon law was studied in a disciplined fashion at the mediaeval universities, Oxford and Cambridge. That justifies us in taking the two laws, common and civil, as interacting and even complementary. This observation helps Wormald to identify four 'stimuli' which encouraged rulers to accept judicial responsibilities.

> Foremost among these was the example of God's holy people [the Old Testament Israel/Judah]. A second was the general sense that that other people of destiny, the Romans, specialized in the art of law as in that of war. Third was an awareness that an early medieval people was identified by its law. Last, pulling all four together, was the growing feeling that royal law should look like the Learned Laws of God's Church and Rome's Empire. Such forces might prompt intense legalistic activity before they urged any final commitment to written law. In early England they did.[28]

Whereas in Southern Europe the survival of the Roman notarial system guaranteed the professionalism of written

[28] Ibid., p. 143.

law, in England that was hardly the order of the day until after the Conquest. Anglo-Saxon law books were heavily adulterated by what such Europeans would doubtless consider extraneous matter. Alfred's 'doombook' was planned as an 'epitome of God's Covenant with the people to whom He had given lowland Britain'.[29] It was not surprising, then, that the homilies of Archbishop Wulfstan were bound in with the same codices, nor that laws so viewed could be inserted into liturgical books, including Gospel-books. So the 'extraneous' religious matter was evidently not accidental.

One can see the chain of argument implied. Liberty is unthinkable without the bonds of law; such bonds imply solidarity in a common moral and spiritual substance; from where does this arise in a Christian commonwealth if not from the Gospel of God?

A thousand years later, in *Fors Clavigera* for September 1875, John Ruskin could be found attacking W. E. Gladstone's concept of freedom. 'Liberty', says Ruskin with not untypical exaggeration, 'whether in the body, soul or political estate of man, is only another word for Death … the body, spirit and political estate being alike healthy only by their bonds and laws; and by Liberty being instantly disengaged into mephitic vapour'.[30] The *manner* in which Ruskin exaggerates becomes clear in hearkening to some words of Maurice Reckitt, one of the Anglo-Catholic founders of the 'Christian Sociology' movement in the years around the Second World War.

[29] Ibid., p. 481.
[30] Cited T. Hilton, *John Ruskin* (New Haven and London), p. 650.

> There are discernible … certain elements in the political and social life of pre-Reformation England which would seem to be enduring characteristics of her make-up and have persisted here, though they have largely decayed elsewhere in Europe. Among the most notable is a strong emphasis on the rule of Law, going together with a readiness to recognize certain widely extended, positive, and specific privileges or 'liberties' – liberty, that is, for the pursuit of a corporate social function rather than liberty from restraint.[31]

Gladstone had represented classical Liberalism which at any rate at his hands – not a philosophical Utilitarian in the school of J. S. Mill but a High Church Anglican – was a good deal less noxious than much of what we find a century on. The modern intolerant, lobby-driven, issue-obsessed cultural liberalism (obnoxious by its itchy interferingness even to the disciples of Mill) is a very different kettle of fish. The capacity for national self-determination and for democractic accountability (two real goods identified by classical Liberalism) appears to be eroding under the pressure of imposed multi-culturalism – as distinct from the possible bi-culturalism I advocated in chapter one above – as well as an internationalism of an exaggerated kind.[32] But law is too important to be made the instrument of political correctness.

Law should indeed restrain evil – though on certain presuppositions, the counting of some features of human

[31] M. B. Reckitt, 'Catholic Sociology and the English Situation', in idem., *Prospect for Christendom. Essays in Catholic Social Reconstruction* (London 1945), p. 93.

[32] See D. Conway, *In Defence of the Realm. The Place of Nations in Classical Liberalism* (Aldershot 2004).

behaviour as evil because contrary to justice may be misdescribed: for example, is the non-selection of gay adoption parents discriminatory and therefore unjust? But law must also promote the good, commending those who do right. (Compare, when you have a moment, the words of the apostles in The Letter to the Romans 13, 3-4, and The First Letter of Peter 2, 14.) Overall, it is the failure of historic liberalism that it has preferred to avoid evil rather than seek the good.[33] Thus the most celebrated re-statement of liberalism in our time, John Rawls' *A Theory of Justice*,[34] abjures judgments on what sorts of lives are good.

The heirs of the 'Coming of Christianity to Anglo-Saxon England' can hardly be expected to sleep easy with so fastidious a withdrawal from the effort of discerning the virtues.[35] Influence on law of liberalism of this sort can only corrode what is left of the bonds that held together an English Christendom so early apparent in the Lindisfarne Gospel-book, as in that Christendom's civil society and State.

The crown: from sacred canopy to 'anomie'

In this section what I am concerned with is not 'the Crown' in the wider constitutional sense – the legal entity the overwhelming majority of whose executive powers and prerogatives are wielded by ministers in

[33] P. Manent, *An Intellectual History of Liberalism* (English translation Princeton, NJ, 1995), pp. 3-38.
[34] J. Rawls, *A Theory of Justice* (Oxford 1999, revised edition; original, 1971). For a critique which retains elements of a more classical view, J. Raz, *The Morality of Freedom* (Oxford 1986).
[35] The reference is to the magisterial study by Henry Mayr-Harting, *The Coming of Christianity to Anglo-Saxon England* (London 1991, 3rd edition).

Cabinet government. If there were ever a second English Republic, these powers and prerogatives would remain, though to be re-assigned. Rather, I am concerned with the monarchy proper, and specifically the issue of the reinvigoration of the monarchical symbol, which is the true centre of unity for the life of civil society in the island of Britain.

David Jones, whom I mentioned in my opening chapter, wrote in 1953 of 'the figure who, this summer, by specific acts and things done to her has herself been made the visible sign of that invisible thing, the concept, the Monarchy of Britain'.[36] That referred of course to the Coronation of Elizabeth II. As Jones emphasised, the monarchy necessarily comprises a 'severality' since the peoples she embodies are several – and have become more so, if we think of the significant minorities who have entered the country since that time. In fact, unlike the sceptre, which is older than the crown, the crown (as object) stands for the monarch's role as head of society rather than that limited aspect of society we call 'the State'.

The Coronation ceremony is of the highest importance for the symbolic ordering of the realm. It is the enactment of a solemn covenant between monarch and people. Some few aspects from the last Coronation may be mentioned since in their own symbolic guise they communicate what sort of civil society and State this is meant to be. For the most part, its rituals are transparent. They are readily decoded.[37]

---

[36] D. Jones, 'Wales and the Crown', in idem., *Epoch and Artist* (London 1959), pp. 39-48 and here at p. 40.

[37] H. Thurston, S.J., *The Coronation Ceremonial. Its True History and*

In June 1953, its last occurrence, how did it unfold? Immediately preceding Queen Elizabeth on her entry into Westminster Abbey, were ceremonial bearers of three swords: the 'Sword of Justice to the Temporality' with its sharp point, the 'Sword of Justice to the Spirituality' with its obtuse point, and the 'Sword of Mercy', with its point broken off. The Sword of State, which represents the universal protection of the realm and also the law, came only after these. Notice how mercy and justice (equity – not simply the observance of *de facto* laws) come first. That was, incidentally, the point at issue between James II and Parliament, in the Declaration of Indulgence and other acts of the reign of the last Catholic king.

Meanwhile (reverting to the Abbey on June 2nd) the 'great regalia' had been distributed by their custodians, the dean and prebendaries of Westminster, to various lords of Parliament. Those regalia consisted of a variety of objects: the spurs, the orb, the sceptre, the rod, the staff, and the crown of St Edward. In that moment the supreme authority was temporarily lodged in the hands of Parliament, descendant of the Anglo-Saxon 'witenagemot', council of the wise, out of which Parliament – notably in the Upper House – has grown. But the Queen was there to seek a higher title than earthly Parliaments can give. So all the regalia were handed over for a while to the Archbishop of Canterbury.

It is a defensible interpretation of the rite, at any rate in the intention of its original framers, to say that when

Meaning (London 1902) gives the text, as restored after various mutilations, and some background.

the Queen rose from praying at the 'Chair of Estate', all power in the realm had been given for one moment into the keeping of the Church. That is why it fell to the Archbishop to present the Queen to those assembled, asking whether they were willing to do her homage and service. The Queen acknowledged their response, 'God save Queen Elizabeth', by curtseys because as yet, before her anointing, her royalty was 'sacramentally' (in an extended sense of the word, a post-Tridentine Catholic would say) as yet incomplete.[38]

For what follows I quote from *The Times* for Wednesday June 3rd, 1953:

> But before the rites could be lifted to the sacramental level there was a reminder of the stark contractual basis upon which this mystical marriage of Church and State rests. Having the plenitude of power in his possession, the Archbishop could make terms for its bestowal. Standing before the Chair of Estate, he asked the Queen whether she was willing to take the Oath, and, she having replied 'I am willing', proceeded to require of her the ancient promises to govern all her peoples – now separately named – according to their respective laws and customs, to cause justice and mercy to be executed in all her judgments, and to maintain the profession of the Gospel, the privileges of the clergy, and in the United Kingdom the Protestant reformed religion established by law. Having solemnly promised to do all these things, the Queen rose and followed the Sword of State to the altar, where, kneeling on

[38] The question whether the anointing of kings should count as a sacrament was only decided definitively (in the negative) at the sixteenth-century Council of Trent.

> the steps, and with her hand upon the Bible, open at the Gospel of St John, she confirmed her promise with a solemn oath, a copy of which she proceeded to sign.[39]

Then after the singing of the *Veni Creator*, and the Archbishop's recital of a prayer for the Queen's strengthening – said over the 'ampulla', the vessel containing the oil of chrism, the monarch disrobed for her anointing on the hands, breast and head, under a cloth of gold canopy.

Hitherto, the Church had held the emblems of temporal authority since there was no one spiritually qualified to wear and wield them. Now there was such a person and the investiture could begin. The Dean of Westminster put on her the white *colobium sindonis*, or alb, and the gold *super-tunica*, comparable in form to the deacon's dalmatic, but held at the waist by a golden sword-belt. The spurs of St George, the protector of the realm, were brought to her to touch (a male monarch would have them applied to his feet). Then the jewelled sword which substitutes for this purpose for the Sword of State was given to the Queen by the Archbishop (and the other bishops) who adjured her to use it with justice, stop the growth of iniquity, protect the holy Church of God, and defend widows and orphans. Next, she put on the armills or gold bracelets whose symbolic valency is not historically entirely clear, but at the coronation of Elizabeth II they were described as 'symbols and pledges of that bond which unites you with your peoples' (of

[39] 'In the Abbey', *The Times*, 3 June 1953, p. 11.

the British Commonwealth of Nations, q. v.). Then she received the stole and the robe royal – somewhat like a cope but square, embroidered with various emblems for the parts of the United Kingdom. Taking the orb, surmounted by the cross, she was reminded that 'the whole world is subject to the power and empire of Christ our Redeemer'. The ring – the 'wedding ring of England' – which represents the ring St Edward the Confessor gave to an aged beggar who later revealed himself as St John the Divine, was put on her hand as 'the seal of catholic faith'. The sceptre, the supreme symbol of royal power, the 'ensign of kingly power and justice', was handed over simultaneously with the dove-headed rod, as a sign that justice and mercy are never to be put asunder. The crown itself was then blessed and placed on the sovereign's head by the Archbishop.

Now the Queen left St Edward's chair to move across to the throne to take 'seisin' (possession) of her dominions – ascending the steps, with the hands of spiritual and temporal lords (Canterbury and Norfolk) placed under her elbows she was 'lifted' by the combined power of Church and State onto the seat of the throne. There followed the homage of the bishops, the temporal lords, and the general acclamation, 'God save Queen Elizabeth'. Thus ended the coronation rite proper (itself enclosed in a celebration of the Anglican Communion service).

From this complex and fascinating drama of statecraft we can at least note three things (apart from wondering how much will survive in the coronation of Charles III). The first is the nexus of relations which the crown – and so the crown-bearer – represents, and the rich fashion in which they commit monarch and subjects to a variety of virtues pertinent to the making of a commonwealth: an ordered, participatory society. The second is the important role played by consent. It was a commonplace of mediaeval thought that, with the exception of the chosen people, Israel/Judah, the most immediate origin of the authority of the State is found in the consent of the governed. And thirdly, there can never be an absolute version of sovereignty where there is built in, as here, so highly desirable a tension between the powers of Church and State. In pre-Reformation Western Catholicism, the necessary reference of any 'national' church to the Holy See at Rome rendered that tension inescapable. Unfortunately, in the Henrician and Elizabethan reformations, on which more anon, the quasi-autonomy of the *sacerdotium* vis-à-vis the *regnum* effectively disappeared. In a Catholic perspective, this undermines somewhat the force of the symbolic message offered at coronation time – even though, or perhaps because, in the contemporary period the powers and prerogatives of the Crown are exercised by ministers, notably the Prime Minister, who need not be a Christian at all.

Meanwhile it should be pointed out that the Coronation Oath is an explicit denial of the secularity of the United Kingdom. Constitutionally, this realm remains a Christian country, and that will remain so until there is intentional constitutional change to the contrary. The bonds of the social covenant are still meant to be under God, in the light of the Gospel.

The disparity with the modern legislation, aimed at social engineering, characteristically initiated by 1960s 'permissiveness', is striking. Even more so is the contrast with contemporary individualism and atomism, to which, under the heading, 'The needs of the nation', we shall return in Chapter 3.

Parliament: from council of the wise to party contest

The origins of Parliament lie immemorially hidden in the early Anglo-Saxon age. But the 'council of the wise' subsequently expanded by significant high mediaeval accretions, above all through the additional presence of commoners. The Commons were summoned to Parliament in order to amplify the range of consent to government, especially in matters fiscal. In English constitutional history one can choose at which place to mark the zenith of this institution's functioning. No adjudication on that disputed point will be attempted here. What one can say, however, is that much in the twentieth-century evolution of Parliament has been unfortunate. This is true principally of the House of Commons, by far the more important chamber, but opportunities were also missed more recently for an enhancement of the contributory role of the House of Lords.

So far as the Commons is concerned, the extension of the franchise to all citizens, finally achieved in the extension of the vote to women, fills a lacuna in the concept of the Lower House. The Commons seeks to represent the inhabited territory of the realm: that is why constituencies are geographic. Unfortunately, as the party system bears on this representation, a twentieth-century observer could be forgiven for thinking that:

> the real function of the House of Commons was to serve as a cockpit for a continuous, never-ending struggle between two teams of political gladiators, competing for votes at the next election, and that its older roles as a legislature and as a watchdog over the executive had faded into comparative insignificance.[40]

What of the House of Lords? In the Middle Ages, Parliament represented communities more than it did individuals. In fact, both sorts of representation are desirable. In the modern period, the House of Commons represents, essentially, individuals territorially considered. That is why there is a need for a second chamber that represents functions.

One of the problems with such well-intentioned but short-lived later twentieth-century devices as the 'National Economic Development Council', which sought to harmonise social function by bringing together labour, business, civil servants and ministers, was that no attempt was made to think through the constitutional principles which could have given such entities fuller legitimacy and, therefore, morally suasive power.[41] Perhaps owing to anxieties generated by corporatism in authoritarian polities like Mussolini's Italy, the possibilities of the Upper House of the English Parliament as a 'social chamber' have hardly

[40] D. Marquand, *The Unprincipled Society. New Demands and Old Politics* (London 1988), p. 38.
[41] Ibid., p. 59.

been explored – even though they correspond (in the present writer's opinion) to both contemporary need and historic patrimony.

Under the rubric 'a social chamber', Anglican bishops, and representatives of 'the hereditaries' could sit comfortably – alongside those who would speak for employers and unions, City and professions, and the other faiths. By reason of the Catholic Church's historic importance in our island, as well as its present numbers, and contribution to education, health care and many other facets of life in contemporary England, there should also be in that chamber (not necessarily episcopally) some duly delegated Catholic voices or voice. After all, the innovatory introduction of life peers was not intended merely to reward ex-cabinet ministers and other politicians. It was also meant to bring into Parliament representative examples of those who had distinguished themselves in different walks of life, and could speak for different segments of the social whole. A reorganisation of the Upper House along 'social chamber' lines is the message that the role of this institution in English history would seem to send.

The Church: from Catholic to chimaera

The Church pre-existed England in Roman Britain. For the chief Anglo-Saxon historian, Bede, the Church, both Celtic and Roman, was the essential catalyst in the making of the *gens Anglorum*, the 'people of the English', even if the political unity of the nation belongs outside his own age, with the Anglo-Danish, and the last of the Anglo-Saxon, kings. That Church, whose fortunes in the parochial system and monasticism, the arts and administration, spirituality and scholarship historians trace through the post-Conquest period, entered into crisis as the first third of the sixteenth century drew to a close.

As already mentioned, with the Protestant Reformation – first Henrician-Edwardine and then, after the intermezzo of Mary's reign, Elizabethan – the English Crown (in Parliament or not as the case may be) destroyed the relative autonomy of *sacerdotium* in its relation to *regnum*. In Western Christendom that autonomy had always been guaranteed in principle, however fluctuating it was in practice, by the 'de-centredness' of a national Church which recognised the chief seat of ecclesial authority in the see of Rome. The mutation of relations between Church and State inevitably distorted perception of the more important relation between historically enacted divine transcendence (the Christian revelation) and a particular social, cultural, political community. On the other hand, the Erastian nature of the religious revolt at least preserved the concept that the baptismal faith provides civil society with its foundational form.[42]

The English Reformation was, then, the action of the Crown in establishing control over the Church, far more fully than in the Middle Ages and with a

[42] For the ambiguities of combining the two key Reformation principles of the primacy of Scripture and the primacy of the godly prince, see G. W. Jenkins, *John Jewel and the English National Church. The Dilemmas of an Erastian Reformer* (Aldershot 2006).

systematic repudiation of the claims of the see of Rome. Within this broad(ish) framework much that was Catholic could survive, but in a form vulnerable to theological fashion, political events and – in the setting of mass democracy in the twentieth century – cultural trends. The unity of English Christianity disintegrated in the Tudor period into the three main forms in which we see it today: a State Anglicanism of various stripes, Nonconformist Protestantism ('old Dissenters') and the recusant body which, subsequently amplified by Irish and later Third World economic migration, constitutes the present English Catholic Church.

Was this development a historical necessity? New history writing underlines the way the late mediaeval Church, on the eve of the Reformation, to a degree greater than was commonly recognised later, satisfied the spiritual needs of English men and women. Here the key figures are the Cambridge historian Eamon Duffy,[43] a Catholic, and his Oxford counterpart Christopher Haigh,[44] of Nonconformist background, though these had a harbinger in the Warwick-based J. J. Scarisbrick,[45] also a Catholic. Their studies show that the Protestant aspect of the English Reformation, the dismantlement of the traditional Liturgy and its attendant devotions, as

[43] E. Duffy, *The Stripping of the Altars. Traditional Religion in England, 1400-1580* (New Haven and London 1992); idem., *The Voices of Morebath. Reformation and Rebellion in an English Village* (New Haven and London 2001).

[44] C. Haigh, *English Reformations: Religion, Politics and Society under the Tudors* (Oxford 1993). See also idem. (ed.), *The English Reformation Revised* (Cambridge 1987).

[45] J. J. Scarisbrick, *The Reformation and the English People* (London 1984).

well as the furnishings and accoutrements of the parish church, was profoundly antithetical to the historic Christian sensibility of the English people, formed during a thousand years of Catholic influence. That is what modern Anglo-Catholics had always guessed. Such phenomena as, under Henry VIII, the Pilgrimage of Grace became more difficult to dismiss as politically motivated or otherwise unrepresentative against the rising tide of evidence from wills, churchwardens' accounts, devotional manuals, and commonplace books in the local archives now increasingly tapped. Introducing his book, *The Stripping of the Altars*, Duffy wrote:

> It is the contention of the ... book that late mediaeval Catholicism exerted an enormously strong, diverse and vigorous hold over the imagination and the loyalty of the people up to the very moment of Reformation. Traditional religion had about it no particular marks of exhaustion or decay, and indeed in a whole host of ways, from the multiplication of vernacular religious books to adaptations within the national and regional cult of the saints was showing itself well able to meet new needs and new conditions.[46]

For later Anglo-Catholics in the Church of England this was a two-edged weapon. If popular Catholicism was so serenely successful, what was the need for a break with Rome in the first place? What was left of the claim that the specifically *papal* Catholicism of the late Middle Ages was crying out – in England, at any rate – for purification?

[46] E. Duffy, *The Stripping of the Altars*, op.cit., p. 4.

A second movement of revisionist historiography has also entered the scene. That second movement has as its theme the essentially Protestant nature of the later Reformation in England, and centres on the Oxford Reformation historian and biographer of Cranmer, Diarmaid MacCulloch – formerly an Evangelical Anglican though he now describes himself as a sympathetic observer of Christianity.[47] This is less well known to the educated public, probably because it has hitherto had no one to rival the television presentation skills of Duffy. In any case, it conforms to the settled assumptions of non-Anglo-Catholic Englishmen, unlike the first revisionist movement which challenges them. MacCulloch speaks of the Church of England from at any rate the reign of Edward VI as manifestly a Reformed church on the model of the Continental Reformation. Claims otherwise, driven by a theological urge to emphasise Catholic continuity for the *ecclesia anglicana* across the Reformation divide, are overwhelmingly the creation of the seventeenth and nineteenth centuries.[48]

What MacCulloch calls the 'Anglo-Catholic historiographical victory' in the English universities of the late nineteenth and early twentieth centuries was made possible by the anomalies and compromises of the Elizabethan Settlement but, as to Cranmer, the subject

[47] D. MacCulloch, *The Later Reformation in England, 1547-1603* (Basingstoke 1990; 1992); idem., *Thomas Cranmer. A Life* (New Haven and London 1996); idem., *Tudor Church Militant. Edward VI and the Protestant Reformation* (London 1999; 2001); idem., *Boy King: Edward VI and the Protestant Reformation* (Berkeley, CA, 2002).

[48] Idem., 'The Myth of the English Reformation', *Journal of British Studies* 30 (1991), pp. 1-19.

of MacCulloch's massive biography, 'there was nothing of the via media between Catholicism and Protestantism in Cranmer's plans'. In Cranmer's conflict with Bishop Hooper, the most radical of the Edwardine bishops, the

> point at issue ... was not whether or not the Church of England should retain a Catholic character, but whether or not remnants of the Catholic past could be redirected to Protestant ends, in order to preserve order, decency and hierarchy.[49]

Similar ambiguities continued in Elizabeth's reign, such as the contradiction between the moderate tone of the royal injunctions issued in 1559 and the 'almost simultaneous action of royal commissions of senior Protestant clergy that unleashed a ruthless campaign of systematic vandalism in Church furnishings'.[50] In an earlier generation of scholarship, the Tudor historian John Neale proposed that Elizabeth's government wanted little more than an outward break with Rome, but Protestant activists in the House of Commons forced through a much more thoroughgoing set of changes. Research from the 1980s suggests otherwise. The government got the settlement it desired. Hesitations came from the conservative aristocracy – and of course from the Marian bishops. As MacCulloch notes:

> Whatever the queen's own views, she quickly resigned herself to the inevitability of a thoroughgoing Protestant settlement in 1559, since the only senior clergy prepared to operate a national church for her

[49] Ibid., p. 7.
[50] Ibid., p. 9.

> were convinced Protestants.[51]

MacCulloch's conclusion is that

> Catholic Anglicanism was [thus] at best waiting in the wings when Elizabeth died: a synthesis that had not yet been blended from a mixture of conformist *jure divino* arguments, the Catholic hankerings of a handful of clergy, the rationalism and traditionalism of Hooker and a suspicion of systematic Calvinism.[52]

The situation only changed when under the early Stuarts a diplomatic revolution disposed of English support for Dutch Protestantism, and Laudian clergy gained the mind and heart of Charles I. The consequences were dramatic. As MacCulloch puts it:

> The reaction of the Englishmen who had been nurtured by the Elizabethan church was to overthrow the government which had allowed such a thing to happen; yet when a version of the 1559 religious settlement was restored in 1660, never again was the established church to prove comprehensive enough to contain the spectrum of Protestant belief that had been possible in the late sixteenth century. From this story of confusion and changing direction emerged a church that has never subsequently dared define its identity decisively as Protestant or Catholic and that has decided in the end that this is a virtue rather than a handicap.[53]

That is the ecclesial 'chimaera': a hybrid species, though, as found in the liturgical office of Evensong, in George

[51] Ibid., p. 10.
[52] Ibid., p. 17.
[53] Ibid., p. 19.

Herbert's poetry, in the music of Samuel Sebastian Wesley, certainly not without its beauty – something of which present-day Western Catholics are especially aware, since they have marred much in their own liturgical heritage, giving entry to a philistinism unsuited to the divine glory.

In this book, stating a case for the 'conversion of England', I propose to draw on Anglo-Catholic writers, both in Chapter 4 (notably T. S. Eliot and Chesterton in his Anglican phase) and in Chapter 5 (where Dorothy L. Sayers is a subterraneous presence). Why? Even MacCulloch has to admit that a Catholic party emerged in the Church of England relatively early: certainly, less than seventy-five years after Elizabeth's accession. He is inclined to date it to the moment when, on James I's death, the Duke of Buckingham asked Bishop William Laud to run his finger down a list of senior clergy and set against their names the letters either P or O, meaning 'Puritan' or 'Orthodox'. A High Church tradition was revived at the Stuart Restoration and survived, albeit in ill odour with most governments of the 'Whig Supremacy', throughout the eighteenth century. By the 1830s, it was certainly impossible to say there was no such party – even if, as Sheridan Gilley of the University of Durham has argued, it is

> tempting to trace [the] troubles of the [present day] Church of England to the very nineteenth-century movement which did most for its revival.[54]

[54] S. Gilley, 'The Ecclesiology of the Oxford Movement: a Reconsideration', *Nova* I. 1 (1996), pp. 4-9, and here at p. 4.

Gilley is referring to the Oxford Movement, born as that movement was in the crisis of the European confessional State at the turn of the eighteenth and nineteenth centuries. In Gilley's words, its leaders were 'more than conservatives: they were right-wing radicals who transformed the very tradition they set out to renew'.[55] The 'Apostolicals', as the Oxford men called their party, sought to blow into life the embers of High Anglicanism by arousing an enthusiasm for Western Catholicism even in aspects of its theory and practice hitherto generally rejected.[56] Among these, Hurrell Froude, with his affection for the theocratic mediaeval Church, could be called the founder of Anglican Ultramontanism, a harbinger of the Anglo-Papalism of the most extreme or consistent (depending on how one looks at it) Anglo-Catholicism of the twentieth century.[57] More influentially, the rest of the Oxford Movement men did what their High Church predecessors generally had *not* done: they declared that in possessing the apostolic ministry of bishops to guarantee the sacramental and spiritual life, the Church of England was Catholic and not Protestant. The Anglican *via media* was not the 'old High Anglican Protestant middle way between popery and radical Protestantism'. Rather, Anglicanism,

[55] Ibid., p. 5. The evidence is laid out in Gilley's prosopographical study of Newman in relation to his contemporaries, the distinguishing feature of his biography of the Servant of God: thus S. Gilley, *Newman and his Age* (London 1990).

[56] For the difference the Tractarians made, see P. Nockles, *The Oxford Movement in Context* (Cambridge 1994).

[57] See M. Yelton, *Anglican Papalism. An Illustrated History: 1900-1960* (Norwich 2005).

properly understood, was a *via media* between popery and Protestantism itself. In Gilley's words, John Henry Newman

> awakened the Church of England from the condition in which it could blithely assume that it was both Protestant and Catholic by asking the question which has plagued it ever since: is it essentially Catholic *or* Protestant *or* Liberal?[58]

But just by calling itself Catholic rather than Protestant the Oxford Movement awoke folk fears of Rome (and contributed, along with the Irish immigration, to reviving a hostility to the Recusant community that was otherwise beginning to wither away). By setting out to appropriate the devotional life and discipline of contemporary Catholicism its followers appeared to be not so much interpreting the Book of Common Prayer as supplanting it. Many informed Protestants came to distrust Newman's appeal to the Fathers, implicit in the new 'Library of the Fathers', and his appeal to the more Catholic writers of the Anglican tradition, explicit in the new 'Library of Anglo-Catholic Theology'. Though Anglicanism had long been in Gilley's memorable phrase an 'ecclesiological Noah's Ark', what was novel in the early Victorians was the sharpness of the ensuing self-definition of factions, 'partisan and even warring positions'. The older Protestant High Churchmen were marginalised as Anglican Protestantism became an anti-Anglo-Catholic Evangelicalism, and High Churchmanship an anti-Protestant Anglo-Catholicism.

[58] S. Gilley, 'The Ecclesiology of the Oxford Movement: a Reconsideration', art. cit., p. 5.

A few notable High Anglicans such as W. E. Gladstone retained a strong element of Protestantism in their Anglican Catholicism but the general tendency of Anglo-Catholicism was towards a repudiation of the Protestant inheritance.

Anglo-Catholics could now survive and prosper only by flouting constituted authority. Theoretically, they had adopted an exalted theology of the monarchical episcopate owed to St Ignatius of Antioch and St Cyprian in the early Church. In practice, they defied Protestant and Liberal bishops *con bravura*. Secure in the 'parsons' freehold', they established:

> an infallible priest-Pope in every parish, loyal not to his immediate bishop but to Catholic Christendom in some vaguer, wider sense.[59]

There we have them: on the ascendant from about 1870 to 1940 and then on the decline – and either way, beyond a doubt as to doctrine, worship and devotion though not ecclesial communion, a displaced portion of Catholic Christendom. It is as such that I shall be appealing to some of their lay spokesmen.

The fragile nature of the Anglo-Catholic experiment is obvious, given the minoritarian character of the Catholic movement within the Church of England as a whole. Gilley would go further. On his analysis, the party system created in the later nineteenth century, with theological colleges teaching diametrically opposed Catholic and Protestant theologies, could in the long term benefit

[59] Ibid., p. 7.

> only theological liberalism, for it made the defining character of Anglicanism neither Protestantism nor Catholicism but a liberal comprehensiveness including them both and claiming to be broader, more inclusive, than either.

Appeal to comprehensiveness dilutes both Catholic and Protestant dogma, so that:

> In the end neither Protestants nor Catholics but the theological liberals have proved the victors in the war for the soul of the Church of England.[60]

Yet even at its heyday, around the First World War, Anglo-Catholicism could never have captured the Church of England without the altogether unlikely connivance of the political establishment. That is a consequence of Erastianism. As we have seen, in the Church of England as historically constituted authority belongs essentially to the Crown in Parliament. That reflects the claim of the early Tudor monarchs that England is an 'empire': meaning, that in no respect is there defect in the sovereignty – not only temporal but spiritual – found within the kingdom. The oath all diocesan bishops in the Church of England still swear runs:

> I … lately … having been elected, confirmed and consecrated bishop of … do hereby declare that your majesty is the only Supreme Governor of this your realm in spiritual and ecclesiastical things as well as in temporal, and that no foreign prelate or potentate has any jurisdiction within this realm, and I acknowledge the said bishopric, as well the spiritualities as the temporalities thereof only of your majesty, and for the

60 Ibid.

> same temporalities I do my homage present to your majesty, so help me God.

In the later nineteenth century, when in the first stirrings of response to Anglican Modernism the idea was mooted of a world-wide council of Anglican bishops with authority to judge disputed questions of doctrine, government and discipline, Archbishop C. T. Longley of Canterbury demurred on grounds which included the damage such a council might do to the lawful authority of the Crown in Parliament. The merely consultative gatherings called the 'Lambeth Conferences' were the upshot. Any internal laws provided by the Church of England – whether, in the past, through the Convocations of Canterbury and York, or in the present through the General Synod of the Church of England – remain justiciable by the ordinary courts, since they have to be interpreted in the light of the law of England as such. The reason is: the authority whereby such internal laws are enacted is in the last resort the duly delegated authority of the Crown. No Catholic Christian – the word 'Catholic' means, after all, 'universal' – can accept *ex animo* the merely national Christianity thus implied. Nations are called to act and to be sanctified within the framework of the catholicity of the universal Church.

Law, crown, Parliament and Church at the end of the 'ancien régime'

Nonetheless, through it all the *ancien régime* survived as a recognisable Christendom society, albeit one distorted by the Erastian mould. As the above paragraphs on the

Church indicate, the end of the English *ancien régime* is dateable to the opening decades of the nineteenth century.[61] (Paradoxically, Catholic Emancipation, itself driven by anxiety over Ireland, was key to the emergence of the new settlement.) The Christendom society, first in Catholic and then Anglican form, whose beginnings the Lindisfarne Gospels celebrate, did not terminate, however, in a revolutionary fashion. That is why, unlike the French, we can espouse the truths found in counter-revolutionary literature without turning our backs on the constitutional or ideological history of our country.

Edmund Burke's writings are an example, as are those of T. S. Eliot. (I shall be looking to the latter in Chapter 4.) In the *Reflections on the Revolution in France* Burke expresses his detestation of the 'new political Men of Letters', the urbanised clerisy of *philosophe* publicists who in their purported critique of feudal injustice and ecclesiastical repression brought about a despotism that was far worse. With reason the polymathic literary critic George Steiner speaks of Burke's warranted and 'profound distrust of voluntarist, cerebrally inspired innovations in the inherited weave of communal life'.[62] With considerable prescience in the comparatively benign lull of 1790, Burke saw that, to cite Steiner again:

> Freed from the constraints of religion and social hierarchy, the 'lust of selfish will', the anarchic play

[61] J. C. D. Clark, *English Society, 1688-1832: Ideology, Social Structure and Political Practice during the Ancien Régime* (Cambridge 1985).
[62] G. Steiner, 'Aspects of Counter-Revolution', in G. Best (ed.), *The Permanent Revolution. The French Revolution and its Legacy, 1789-1989* (London 1988), pp. 129-153 and here at p. 135.

> of intellectuality and of material greed, must bring on the regime of the mob. It, in turn, compels the establishment of a dictatorship based, solely, on the spurious legitimacy of the gun. Intuitive, fuelled by metaphor, contemptuous of any such empty concept as that of 'laws of history' or 'economic determinism', Burke's exposition was wholly prophetic; he saw Bonapartism coming out of the very matrix of what looked, in 1790, to be a gradual ripening towards constitutional monarchy and the rule of law.[63]

Burke reiterates the spiritual goals which civil society – and by implication the State – must serve. In a justly celebrated passage of his *Reflections* Burke wrote:

> Society ... is not a partnership for things subservient only to the gross animal existence of a temporary and perishable nature. It is a partnership in all science; a partnership in all art; a partnership in every virtue, and in all perfection. As the end of such a partnership cannot be obtained in many generations, it becomes a partnership not only between those who are living, but between those who are living, those who are dead, and those who are to be born.[64]

As Steiner comments, picking up some phrases of Burke's text:

> The authentic 'tree of liberty' is the 'great blossomer' rooted in the mystery and logic of the immemorial. Torn from the earth, that tree will become the dead

[63] Ibid., p. 137.

[64] E. Burke, 'Reflections on the Revolution in France and on the Proceedings in Certain Societies in London relative to that Event: in a Letter intended to have been sent to a Gentleman in Paris, 1790', in *The Works of Edmund Burke* II (London 1901), p. 368.

> firebrand of the terrorist and the *ad hoc* tyrant.[65]

And as Steiner wryly concludes, 'His case is not one which our own times can, with any facility, dismiss'.[66]

Steiner's reason for saying so is that, while the technical abrogation of the English *ancien régime* left intact much of its form and substance, the invasion of political modernity – for which he looks to Goethe (mediated by Friedrich von Schlegel) for description – took its eventual toll.

> Goethe takes the ultimate significance of the French Revolution to be one of *politicization*. An *ancien régime* is one in which ordinary men and women conduct their lives within their social caste, locale and profession. The making, the suffering of history is, in essence, the business of the few. Even as traditional warfare is the business of the aristocrat and the mercenary. What the French Revolution has done is to abolish the millennial barriers between common life and the enormities of the historical. Past the hedge and gate of even the humblest garden march the bayonets of political ideology and historical conflict. The consequence is not only that of a quantum leap in the scale, ferocity and unpredictability of political-historical events: it is a reduction, ontological as well as psychological, in the inner space, in the inner temporality of private being.

And Steiner elucidates Goethe's point:

> The leisure, the fundamental quietude needed for men and women to come to know themselves, the *dignitas*

[65] G. Steiner, 'Aspects of Counter-Revolution', art. cit., pp. 138-139.
[66] Ibid., p. 139.

> of discretion within *domesticity*, are swept away by the ephemeral relevance of public news ... Under stress of political totality, the individual can no longer ripen towards the authenticity of his own private person. And for Goethe ... such ripening outweighs all external liberations.[67]

The invasion of personal life by politically correct programmes of governmental action, the phenomenon of the 'Nanny State', the increasing burden of statutory legislation and regulation, much of it demanded by the overseas bureaucracy at Brussels, are all realities of England at the start of the twenty-first century even if we abstract from the dominating force of an ideology: secular liberalism.

What, then – bearing in mind that salutary warning of the limits set to all social questions by proper respect for the uniqueness and dignity of individual persons – are now the real needs of the nation?

[67] Ibid., p. 143.

Chapter 3

The Needs of the Nation

The nation

Contrary to a popular scholarly misconception, nations are real and they cannot easily be de-constructed. There can indeed be an element of deliberate planning and human creativity in their formation – or re-formation (in fact this book is one example of an imaginative version thereof). But that is not to say that nations are a recent creation, typically engendered – so the influential speculations of Ernest Gellner would have it – in the modern (late eighteenth century) transition from spontaneous, non-literate 'low' cultures to highly cultivated, literate and specialised 'high' cultures, as an intelligentsia invites the masses into history.[68] Nations are also, in the words of Anthony Smith, 'the products of traditions and heritages which have coalesced over generations'. And Smith goes on:

> What the modernists [i.e. those who trace the idea of the nation no further than the modern period] often overlook is the persistence of ethnic ties and cultural sentiments which in some cases date back to pre-modern times.[69]

And Smith points out that the first nations in Western Europe, England among them, are examples of this, and such nations 'acted as models and pioneers of the idea of

[68] E. Gellner, *Nations and Nationalism* (Oxford 1983).

[69] A. Smith, 'Gellner on Nationalism', *Prospect* (December 1995), p. 19.

the nation for others'.

The nation is not the State. The State is, simply, a relatively higher power within the network of authorities that constitute the body politic. It is not a separate and transcendent power entitled to act upon the body politic in any way it wishes. In his 1951 essay *Man and the State*, the Thomist political philosopher Jacques Maritain stigmatised the contrary of this view as 'substantialism': the myth that the State is the people personified.[70] In calling the true doctrine of the State an 'instrumental' one, Maritain meant, in the words of his later American disciple Russell Hittinger, that

> the apparatus of public law is an instrument serving the rights and liberties of various societies, which, together, form a whole that cannot be equated with the state.[71]

'The state', Hittinger continues, 'is an instrument of different modes of solidarity; it is neither the substance nor the exemplar of society.'[72] This viewpoint is echoed in *Gaudium et spes*, the Pastoral Constitution of the Second Vatican Council on the Church in the Modern World, which insists that the function of public authority is not to determine the character of the civilization proper to its civil society, but rather to establish conditions conducive to the life of culture and use means capable of fostering it. Is this, then, a rejection of any genuinely *corporate* notion of the State – a natural one to those

[70] J. Maritain, *Man and the State* (English translation Chicago 1952).

[71] R. Hittinger, *The First Grace. Rediscovering the Natural Law in a Post-Christian World* (Wilmington, Delaware, 2002), p. 265.

[72] Ibid., p. 266.

whose imaginations are still informed by the notion of a covenanted people under a king? We must recall that not all notions of kingship are absolutist, nor are all modern corporate views of the State invasive of due liberties.

Based upon charters, customs and local privileges the ancient constitution of England preserved plural authorities, and had considerable resources for resisting centralisation. It is a question of building on this, to move toward a society that multiplies associative authorities without usurping the place that properly belongs to law-making authorities, whether civil or ecclesiastical. These associative authorities are there to defend various civic goods. Speaking up for rights of association by working men, Pope Leo XIII, at the end of the nineteenth century, drew this kind of argumentation from Thomas Aquinas's defence of the Dominicans against the secular clergy in his treatise *Contra impugnantes.*[73] Similar notions are found exactly one hundred years later in Pope John Paul II's 1991 encyclical *Centesimus annus* which commemorates and updates Leo's ground-breaking letter, *Rerum novarum.* In *Centesimus annus* the Polish pope spoke of 'intermediate communities [that] exercise primary functions and give life to specific networks of solidarity'.[74] It is part of the ontological perfecting of our nature that common goods – indeed, the common good in its totality – should be achieved, where possible, by free collaborative agency, at every level from the family to the State.

[73] Leo XIII, *Rerum novarum*, 37.

[74] John Paul II, *Centesimus Annus*, 49.

An objective common good

Not that some theologically neutral democratic consensus based simply on a recognition of the dignity of man will suffice by itself to construct – either in theory or in reality alike – an adequate common good. As divergence over, for example, the issue of abortion shows, such simple humanism is too flimsy a foundation when so many different philosophical readings of it are possible – and influence what the ethicist Alasdair MacIntyre calls 'plain pre-philosophical persons'. Rather, the common good needs foundations in commonly acknowledged moral, and ultimately spiritual, truth. In other words, we are talking about an *objective* common good.

> [A] 'theoretically neutral' consensus inevitably brings about a transformation of the religious convictions of its citizens from publicly relevant, supremely important guides for thought and action, into mere public bulwarks for the 'more important' public values of the democratic faith. Since the democratic charter, representing the sole blueprint for the production and maintenance of the public good, rests upon no particular philosophical or religious creed ... and [despite its original evangelical inspiration] retains its integrity and strength precisely because it eschews a metaphysical and religious foundation, then it would follow ... that religiously relevant political prescriptions would be rendered inane at best, and dangerous at worst, in the hearts and minds of the citizenry.[75]

[75] T. Kozinski, 'Jacques Maritain's "Democratic Faith" – Sound Catholic Philosophy?', *The Latin Mass* (Winter 2004), pp. 10-16 and here at p. 14.

That is, of course, the conviction of secularists in Britain today. The public square must be swept clean of religious detritus. But the de-construction in the name of democratic neutralism of the sacred canopy of a Christendom State, brings with it baleful consequences for the religion of the Incarnation, where the Word, taking flesh, seeks embodiment in human culture – in all the forms human creativity takes, of which the political is one. Indeed, for Catholic Christians active participation in such an order

> would tend to habituate one into privatizing his truth claims, first in public but then in private, such that religious indifferentism or apathy would result.

That is, surely, a major factor in the ecclesial apathy identified in the opening chapter of this book as a major cause of Church decline. Chasing religion from the scene of public life, so the Polish-American commentator Thaddeus Kozinski concludes, would entail an

> enforced divorce of one's deep, comprehensive worldview from political life inasmuch as one is told in countless ways ... that such a divorce is rendered morally obligatory by the exigencies of pluralism ...[76]

And where, then, does that leave, he asks, the 'social reign of Christ the King' – which in the English context, we may take as the nineteenth and early twentieth-century Catholic motif that tries to render into prose one major aspect of the symbolic drama of the English coronation ritual: life in society under the Gospel of God.

This dilemma furnished the besetting weakness of

[76] Ibid.

post-Second World war Christian Democracy in Europe. The likely consequences of prolonged habituation to an order where devotion to the publicly celebrated, legally enforced and socially respectable democratic faith is obligatory, while devotion to the publicly neglected, legally ignored and socially eschewed religious faith is voluntary, are – the grace of God aside – obvious. The later Maritain, the great exponent of a consciously non-sacral Christian Democracy, ruefully admitted that without widespread reverence for spiritual goods it would not work. Is that necessary pre-condition verified in the early twenty-first-century West? We think not. For the Maritain of 'Integral Humanism',[77] the inspiration of the Gospel in a post-Christendom order would inevitably stimulate moral progress even among those who failed to confess the truth the Gospel embodies. That is scarcely credible. If true, there would be required no communication of divine wisdom, and no Church teaching activity, for right morals appropriate to the Incarnation era to be everywhere enjoined. If Pope John Paul II was correct in saying in his first, programmatic, encyclical *Redemptor hominis* that the revelation of Jesus Christ is the only mirror in which man can comprehend himself, how can it be possible to assert that civil society can prescind from its ultimate end?[78] Temporal welfare

[77] J. Maritain, *True Humanism* (English translation London 1938). The phrase cited is taken from the title of the French original: *Humanisme intégral* (Paris 1936).

[78] This question forms in effect the starting-point of David Schindler's comparison of the contemporary Western civil order with the anthropology proper to revelation in his *Heart of the World, Center of the Church. Communio Ecclesiology, Liberalism and Liberation* (Edinburgh 1996).

implies an ordering to the spiritual and supernatural, and individual citizens are directly bound to tend to it.

Maritain's situation in the France and North America of the years immediately before and after World War Two excuses, up to a point, his blindness to the drawbacks of pluralism. Today in England, the emergence at one end of the spectrum of a scientific elite careless of ethics (compare the proposed licensing in the United Kingdom, in the year of writing, 2007, of hybridised human and non-human animals, at least to the age of fourteen days) and at the other end the existence of a radically alienated minority among Muslims seeking the establishment in the United Kingdom of the Sharia law, tends to make one rather more aware of what is involved.[79]

In 1946 Victor Gollancz wrote a study, *Our Threatened Values*, which is still pertinent since the England of the early twenty-first century remains comparable with the England of the post-Second World War world. Desirable the analysis may be, but the very title is enough to make contemporary libertarians shudder. Likewise or more so, orthodox Catholics commenting on the 'state of the realm' can be expected to sound antediluvian. But, seen in a certain perspective, this may be more a badge of honour than of shame. In his analysis of British political culture, the political scientist David Marquand

[79] As Robert Song puts it: 'There is much that is attractive about Maritain's new Christendom and the Thomist understanding of the person and society which grounds it. However, … his reading of Aquinas serves to justify a version of political liberalism only through a tacit historical relativism and historicism': thus his *Christianity and Liberal Society* (Oxford 1997), p. 131. For Song the deficiencies might be resolved by placing Maritain's theory in an Augustinian framework.

wrote by way of an historical retrospect of his own:

> Britain had become the pathfinder in the first place because she had broken more decisively than any other country in the world with the values and assumptions of what Harold Perkin has called the 'Old Society'. The notions that property has duties as well as rights, that consumers owe producers a just price while producers owe consumers just dealing, that the community is a whole greater than the sum of its parts, that high and low are bound together by a chain of reciprocal obligation, that man is placed on earth by God to serve greater ends than the satisfaction of his own wants – all these were victims of a cultural revolution, which preceded and made possible the industrial revolution.[80]

As Marquand points out, the continuing effects of an individualism which he ascribes to the influence of Benthamite Utilitarianism, creates huge difficulties for any account of public purpose (and, we may add, historic spiritual identity). Indeed:

> In a political culture shaped by the assumption that society is made up of separate, atomistic individuals, pursuing only their own private purposes, the notion of a public purpose which is more than the sum of private purposes is apt to seem dangerous, or meaningless, or both.[81]

As the nostalgia of the older generation for the years of the Second World War indicates, wartime patriotism

[80] D. Marquand, *The Unprincipled Society. New Demands and Old Politics* (London 1988), p. 7, citing H. Perkin, *The Origins of Modern English Society, 1780-1880* (London 1972), pp. 17-62.
[81] D. Marquand, *The Unprincipled Society*, op. cit., pp. 10-11.

provided something notably absent in peacetime – a sense not only of solidarity embracing all classes and groups but a truly civic (rather than individual) morality as such.

Government is the custodian of the general interest of the community. But in what can that 'general interest' be said to consist? The political parties as currently existing would have a hard job telling us. Conservatives no longer aspire to conserve, and seem agnostic about their fundamental political beliefs. New Labour has little connexion with Labour. Liberal Democrats are enthusiasts for a European Union that is neither liberal (except perhaps in the nineteenth-century Continental sense of anti-clerical) nor democratic. Globalisation, modernisation, inclusion: these catch-all terms of modern politics mean what one wants them to. There has been a dissolution of political value systems even as cynicism has developed about national institutions which have indeed sometimes been tarnished.

It is in this context that the seemingly peripheral issue of the possible disestablishment of the Church of England takes on peculiar importance. One does not have to be an Anglican to be worried by the thought of disestablishment. As Edward Norman – who hovers in something of a limbo between the Anglican and Catholic Churches – avers:

> The symbolical de consecration of the life of a nation is a grave moment in its history, a decisive act of self-evaluation which ought to be taken only after the most profound and philosophical enquiry into the basis of human association. From confessing a higher purpose for human society, even in a very residual manner,

> to regarding its members only as subjects of policing and material welfare, is a very serious matter. Nothing in the existing mode of public debate suggests that consideration of the Disestablishment of the Church – or even broadening the base of Establishment by further inclusions – will be any other than superficial.

And Dr Norman concludes:

> There is no widely accepted theoretical or symbolical alternative to the Christian religion as the justification of public moral consciousness. That is a different thing from saying that Christianity is widely believed in, or that, in a referendum, people would know their best interest. In the latter exigency the members of the public would doubtless 'think for themselves'; would be, as usual, terrified of seeming old-fashioned; would concoct opinions derived from images conveyed by television presentation. Secularisation of the constitution, carried out as a formal constitutional provision, would replace Christianity with the unstated Humanism that is prevalent within the intelligentsia. It is Humanism expressed in a very imprecise fashion, precisely because it is largely undefined. Its lack of a theoretical rendition doubtlessly corresponds with the English *penchant* for pragmatism…[82]

But people need at least to know what are their duties and rights.

Duties and rights

A political community is – compare the ancient laws touched on in Chapter 2 – a web of reciprocal duties

[82] E. Norman, *Secularisation* (London 2003), p. 109.

and rights. We hear today much about the rights, and a good deal less about the duties.[83] The very word ('duty') has come to have a pious, Victorian (or pre-Victorian) ring to it: a dangerous lexical sign. Democracy is not a good when it encourages individuals to treat the political process as a way of maximising self-interest. But the increasing diffusion of an ethos at once egalitarian and individualistic bears this tendency along. In later twentieth-century Britain, the same problem presented itself in terms of common interest organisations like trade unions and professional associations. Where Benthamism prevails such groups tend to pursue the narrow interest of their own clienteles – which are not necessarily the interests of the wider society. And Marquand summarises the political culture that results from these assumptions:

> Politics is about reconciling conflicts between individually chosen purposes. It has no business with the choice of purposes. Indeed, in some versions of this [Benthamite] tradition, the notion that politics might have something to do with the choice of purposes is at least incipiently tyrannical. Freedom means my freedom to choose my own good for myself, and to pursue it in my own way, provided only that I leave others free to choose and pursue their good in their own way. To allow others to take part in the process through which I choose my good would be to allow them to trespass on psychic space which belongs to me – space which it is my right to keep inviolate.[84]

[83] For a powerful attempt to recapture the concept of duty, see D. Selbourne, *The Principle of Duty. An Essay on the Foundations of the Civic Order* (London 1994; 1997).

[84] D. Marquand, *The Unprincipled Society*, op. cit., p. 214.

Yet the public household must surely have some public goods, and some principles on which to give an account of them. In their absence, the draught round the house becomes chilling.

From here Marquand turns to the noted ethicist Alisdair MacIntyre for whom the collapse of the concept of a shared human good means no less than a new Dark Age. For MacIntyre, who may or may not be thinking chiefly of Britain in his remarks, modernity now is reminiscent of the age when

> men and women of goodwill turned aside from the task of shoring up the Roman *imperium* and ceased to identify the continuation of civility with the maintenance of that *imperium*.[85]

Marquand likewise cites Daniel Bell's *Cultural Contradictions of Capitalism* to some effect. The hallmark of our time is the

> loss of *civitas*, that spontaneous willingness to obey the law, to respect the rights of others, to forgo the temptations of private enrichment at the expense of the public weal – in short to honour the 'city' of which one is a member.[86]

Already in the high Victorian age the moral vacuum being created was sensed: such disparate commentators as, for example, Carlyle and Cobbett, Ruskin and Pugin, Dickens and the young Disraeli, have this in common.

Summarising much of the domestic policy history

[85] A. MacIntyre, *After Virtue. A Study in Moral Theory* (London 1985, 2nd edition), p. 263.
[86] D. Bell, *The Cultural Contradictions of Capitalism* (London 1979, 2nd edition), p. 245.

of the British polity in the twentieth century, Marquand concludes:

> In Britain ... the reaction against full-blooded market liberalism took place under the same philosophical aegis as the movement towards it. Contemporaries, anxious to come to grips with the changes through which they were living, naturally made much of the differences between the 'Collectivism' of the end of the nineteenth century and the 'Individualism' of the beginning. What stands out in retrospect is the continuity between the two. State intervention was tentative, hesitant and reactive; and although it was sometimes justified in other terms, the logic behind it was essentially utilitarian. Moreover, [as already mentioned] the private producer groups which increasingly 'distorted' the free market shared the individualistic ethos which had paved the way for the market economy and helped to inspire its apologists.[87]

Over against the atomism and anomie, can the Catholic tradition – which, in line with the remarks on Anglo-Catholicism offered above, I interpret to include the Catholic-compatible component in the Church of England – serve our need?

[87] D. Marquand, *The Unprincipled Society*, op. cit., p. 223.

Chapter 4

CRITICS OF THE CULTURE

The most signal Catholic contribution to the definition of culture in England belongs with the middle decades of the twentieth century. It emanated from two inter-related circles: one, London-oriented, around Christopher Dawson of whom the Anglo-Welsh poet and artist David Jones was a notably original disciple, and the other, Oxford-based, around J. R. R. Tolkien. Both had important filaments of connexion to the Anglo-Catholic intellectuals of the period, notably T. S. Eliot (and via Eliot, in the significant past, S. T. Coleridge), as well as Charles Williams, Dorothy Sayers, and – in the mode of 'mere Christianity' – C. S. Lewis: the woman among them will appear in Chapter 5. For both Catholic and Anglo-Catholic, Jacques Maritain was a major influence, and the project of the re-launching *in some form* of a Christendom society – on the grounds not least that, in modern circumstances, this alone could salvage good paganism – a common task. Though they would have hated the idea of an intelligentsia, one should also include G. K. Chesterton and Hilaire Belloc as major figures: they too were 'public moralists' of their age.

The pace of this essay will slow here: the change of tempo is needed so as to overcome that characteristic incubus of the 1960s, the inability to say anything much coherent or continuous about experience. To my mind, these figures are as much sages as they are critics. They offer wisdom, a discrimination about life. That is how from evangelical resources, both revelatory and rational, they can be not simply 'critics of culture' but socially regenerative figures. After all:

> A culture is an enhancement of the human being who lives within it or a debasement, according to the discrimination which the culture encourages or limits.[88]

Eliot, Coleridge, Arnold

Probably the best way in is via Eliot. In his 'primer of modern heresy', *After Strange Gods*, appeal is made to, among others, Chestertonian Distributism, Dawson's *The Making of Europe*, and the Anglican 'Christendom sociologists' (Maurice Reckitt, already cited, Vigo Auguste Demant, and their colleagues).[89] Eliot looked back also to two nineteenth-century masters of English literature who shared his concern not only with literary criticism but with social criticism too. And these were Samuel Taylor Coleridge and Matthew Arnold. Coleridge was by far the more kindred spirit, at any rate after Eliot's Baptism. There is a parallel between Eliot's hostility to Communism and Coleridge's to Jacobinism: among other things, both men thought it folly to locate the key to virtue and happiness in *forms of government*

---

[88] H. Grisewood, *The Painted Kipper*, op. cit., p. 10.

[89] V. A. Demant, *God, Man and Society* (London 1933); idem., *Christian Polity* (London 1936); idem., (ed.), *Our Culture: its Christian Roots and Present Crisis* (London 1947).

alone.[90] (Thus for example in England today, the single greatest social problem – the collapse of family structure and discipline – can hardly be solved by the State, even though some government action, such as altering the system of taxation to favour the family, could help up to a point.) More positively, both Eliot and Coleridge considered that Christian thought in England could be revitalised, for which purpose the formation of a Christian intelligentsia – Coleridge's famous 'clerisy' – was a precondition.

In Coleridge's use, notably in *On the Constitution of the Church and State* (1829), written in the death-throes of England's *ancien régime*, a 'clerisy' is an educated religious body which has assumed a sense of public vocation, or mission to civil society. It is, in effect, a re-working of the notion of the clergy as the 'first estate' in a differentiated society of a traditional kind. But the re-working is radical inasmuch as the distinction clergy/laity becomes itself of secondary importance in this context. In *The Idea of a Christian Society* Eliot makes explicit appeal to Coleridge's view – not, however, in the name of a downgrading of the role of ordained ministers as such. The parish system was important to Eliot, as to all observers of how the post-Reformation national church functions in everyday English social life. In the present chapter, I put forward six figures as exemplars of a Coleridgean clerisy: Eliot himself, then David Jones, Christopher Dawson, G. K. Chesterton, J. R. R. Tolkien and Hilaire Belloc. These are critics and sages

[90] R. Kojecky, *T. S. Eliot's Social Criticism* (London 1971), p. 21.

who, as spokesmen for the 'Community of Christians' (Eliot's version of Coleridge's phrase) offer resources for renewing our national life albeit at different levels.

Moreover, like Coleridge, Eliot found the notion of tradition essential to Christianity (as to all social existence worth the name). Both men presented it as an impersonal reality that is itself pro-personal, since, when functioning duly, it fosters the individual and his or her talent.[91] For his part, Coleridge had deemed that collaboration of tradition and the individual to be vital ever since his conversion to Trinitarian Christianity. For a Christian in an ecclesial community dating from the Reformation period – however much it might also refer at times to earlier witnesses – Coleridge held a remarkably high theology of tradition.[92] If society is to find inspiration in ecclesial tradition, then the weightiness of that tradition must be felt.

The magisterial Reformers of the sixteenth century had wanted to minimise the role given to tradition in response to a 'self-interpreting' Word. That was a rejection turned to quite other ends in the rise of a theological liberalism subjectivist in mode. In the (posthumous) *Confessions of an Enquiring Spirit* Coleridge certainly rejected verbal inerrancy in Scripture. But contrary to the picture gained by reading Coleridge through Liberal Protestant spectacles, the Coleridge scholar Jeffrey Barbeau maintains that:

---

[91] A reference to Eliot's essay, 'Tradition and the Individual Talent' (1919), reprinted in idem., *Selected Essays* (London 1951), pp. 13-22.

[92] J. W. Barbeau, 'Coleridge and the "Master-Key" of Biblical Interpretation', *Heythrop Journal* XLV (2004), pp. 1-21.

> [R]ather than arguing for subjectivism in biblical interpretation, Coleridge ... emphasizes the objective sources of revelation expressed in Scripture and the church traditions handed over from the apostles.[93]

Coleridge did not deny that Scripture is a unique vehicle of moral and religious truth, explicitly declaring indeed, that '[e]very sentence found in a canonical Book, rightly interpreted, contains the *dictum* of an infallible Mind'.[94] But he valued tradition 'not merely as a supplement but as a necessary guide that precedes the very formation of the [biblical] canon'.[95] Coleridge presents an oral and catechetical process, shaped by the Church, as a necessary safeguard against private interpretation of Scripture. The credal 'tenets and mysteries' received at Baptism are what 'according to my scheme, every Christian born in Church-membership ought to bring with him to the sacred Scriptures as the master-key of interpretation'.[96] In the absence of a more consistent Catholic ecclesiology – Coleridge acknowledges the interpretative infallibility of no one Church (and specifically repudiates the 'strange mosaic' whereby Roman doctrine has found in Scripture, for example, Purgatory and the Petrine ministry[97]) – one key question is left hanging in the air. How does one identify the orthodox churches to which

[93] Ibid., p. 1.
[94] S. T. Coleridge, *Confessions of an Enquiring Spirit*, ed. D. Jasper (Philadelphia 1988), p. 45.
[95] J. W. Barbeau, 'Coleridge and the "Master-Key" of Biblical Interpretation', art. cit., p. 5.
[96] S. T. Coleridge, *Confessions of an Enquiring Spirit*, ed. D. Jasper, op. cit., p. 45.
[97] Ibid., p. 43.

Coleridge would make appeal? Still, the importance of his emphasis on corporate tradition as the proper context of reading Scripture stands. And that is so even though an 'enquirer' outside the Church might in principle come (so Coleridge thinks) by study of Scripture to esteem and love this body of literature 'formerly viewed by him as a dry stick on a rotten branch, which has *budded* and, like the rod of Aaron, *brought forth buds and blossoms, and yielded almonds*'.[98] The makers of the Lindisfarne Gospel-book would have understood that.

It is easy to see how Coleridge might have inspired Eliot's social theological ideas – and with them his approach to Christianity as a whole. Arnold seems a less plausible candidate. In an essay of 1932 re-published in his 1951 *Selected Essays* Eliot berates Arnold for taking religion to include morals and art but *not thought* – a mistake of which Coleridge, like Eliot himself, could never be guilty.[99] The value of Arnold to Eliot lay chiefly in Arnold's interest in the conditions which favour the play of ideas and the emergence of the best ideas among them. (That Arnold does not actually argue for any *particular* truths or forms makes him for Eliot's purposes a useful agnostic of a mild kind.) Eliot's concept of culture overlaps significantly with that of Arnold, for he often spoke of it in Arnoldian terms as the mental and spiritual life of a society. (In other contexts, Eliot could

[98] Ibid., p. 48. Italics original. See further: R. Barth, *Coleridge and Christian Doctrine* (Cambridge, MA, 1969; reprinted New York 1987); C. Welch, 'Samuel Taylor Coleridge', in N. Smart (ed.), *Nineteenth Century Religious Thought in the West* (Cambridge 1985), 2., pp. 1-28.

[99] T. S. Eliot, 'Arnold and Pater', in idem., *Selected Essays* (London 1951), p. 434.

appeal both to a broader, anthropological, concept of culture than this and to a narrower one: [high] culture as the distinctive contribution of 'urbane' or highly educated citizens.[100])

Eliot was more concerned about the diachronic transmission of culture, its transmission over time, Arnold with its synchronic diffusion – at some given time, but across space – to greater numbers of people. Yet both sought a wider elite, not for its own sake, but so as to benefit the entire community – as Eliot's *Notes towards the Definition of Culture* make plain.[101]

The breadth of Eliot's outlook is especially shown by his striking doctrine of the family. This is not the nuclear family taken by itself, for whose concentration of experienced affection, the smaller it is – so it might seem – the better it can be. The family Eliot favours is the massively inter-generational family (more, anyway, than *three* generations), a family that points to both past and future. Of the family so conceived Eliot wrote: 'Unless this reverence for past and future is cultivated in the home, it can never be more than a verbal convention in the community'.[102]

But where Eliot decisively parted company with Arnold was in nothing less than 'what Arnold wanted

[100] R. Kojecky, *T. S. Eliot's Social Criticism*, op. cit., p. 31.

[101] T. S. Eliot, *Notes towards the Definition of Culture* London 1948; 1962), p. 37. See further, B. Willey, *Nineteenth Century Studies: Coleridge to Matthew Arnold* (London and New York 1949).

[102] T. S. Eliot, *Notes towards the Definition of Culture*, op. cit., p. 44. He added, 'Such an interest in the past is different from the vanities and pretensions of genealogy; such a responsibility for the future is different from that of the builder of social programmes', ibid.

to do'. Eliot defined it in his essay 'The Modern Mind'. Arnold's aim had been to 'preserve emotions without the beliefs with which their history had been involved'.[103] Eliot intended, rather, to preserve valuable emotions by re-pristinating those more foundational beliefs to which the Christian Creed is central. As he put it in *Notes* again:

> Arnold gives the impression that Culture (as he uses the term) is something more comprehensive than religion; that the latter is no more than a necessary element, supplying ethical formation and some emotional colour, to Culture which is the ultimate value.[104]

And yet Eliot, we can say, is highly Arnoldian when he remarks of contemporary Britain:

> [A] growing weakness of our culture has been the increasing isolation of elites from each other, so that the political, the philosophical, the artistic, the scientific, are separated to the great loss of each of them, not merely through the arrest of any general circulation of ideas, but through the lack of those contacts and mutual influences at a less conscious level, which are perhaps even more important than ideas.[105]

Eliot was convinced in fact that a *re-integration of the national culture* was desperately needed. His pleas along these lines gained greater weight from his authority as the Modernist poet who had identified most sharply the

---

[103] Idem., 'The Modern Mind' in *The Use of Poetry and the Use of Criticism* (London 1933), p. 135.
[104] Idem., *Notes towards the Definition of Culture* , op. cit., p. 28.
[105] Ibid., p. 38.

elements of disintegration and loss in early twentieth-century English culture and life.

A critic has remarked of *The Waste Land* of 1922:

> Although the poem seemed to be an attack upon respectable Christian society, it was in reality a lament, and a cry of alarm, over the deliquescence of the civilization of the West: falling into a comfortable materialism, devoid of all authentic Christianity, and with only a sterile respectability left behind. Despite its 'modernist' techniques, … the poem implies a prophetic denunciation of the secularism, rationalism, and materialism characteristic of the modern era. The Waste Land is thus the most notable instance of radically innovative, 'modernist' art in the service of tradition.[106]

As R. V. Young describes the poem, whereas its surface conveys irony and disillusion, its underlying structure is 'mythic': that is, 'it organizes experience in terms of grand, epic narratives', the aim being to disabuse shallow and cynical contemporaries of the attitudes engendered by such 'deadly sins' as pride, lust and sloth.[107] The obliqueness of the mythic references is what gives the poem its difficult Modernist texture, but the references to traditional sources of wisdom – this is a work of Eliot's pre-Christian period – including the Old Testament prophets, the Gospels and Augustine's *Confessions*, as well as Virgil and the Buddha, are unmistakable nonetheless.

---

[106] R. V. Young, 'Withered Stumps of Time: *The Waste Land* and Mythic Disillusion', *The Intercollegiate Review* 38. 2 (2003), pp. 24-32, and here at p. 24.

[107] Ibid., pp. 24, 25.

As Peter Ackroyd has written, in the course of his career Eliot loosened the hold of 'Modernists' on English culture – by arguing for the insufficiency of the Modernist attempt to found a new order based simply on literature and art, with the manifestations of the latter as 'heterocosms', self-contained worlds.

> Not only did [Eliot] assert the public role and 'social usefulness' of the writer in an almost nineteenth-century manner, but he also announced that the principles he derived from his religious belief were more enduring than literary or critical ones. He helped to create the idea of a modern movement with his own 'difficult' poetry, and then assisted at its burial.[108]

Eliot, Maritain, Maurras

The importance, for good or ill, of Jacques Maritain, for any modern Christian re-thinking of 'realms', has already been signalled in Chapter 3. (Thus for instance, Maritain was not omitted from consideration in the single most influential 'middle-of-the-road' Anglican treatise on this subject, Archbishop William Temple's *Christianity and Social Order.*[109]) A good deal in Eliot's personal evolution was owed to the influence of – not so much the 'mature' as – the *early* Maritain, whom he seems to have begun reading in 1926. In 'The Modern Mind' he expressly approved Maritain's view that:

> By showing us where moral truth and the genuine supernatural are situated, religion saves poetry

[108] P. Ackroyd, *T. S. Eliot* (London 1984), p. 239.

[109] W. Temple, *Christianity and Social Order* (London 1950, 3rd edition).

> from the absurdity of believing itself destined to transform ethics and life: saves it from overweening arrogance.[110]

Eliot might not have been so taken by Maritain had he not shared the latter's interest in making accessible in a contemporary idiom the notion of a cultural order where 'literary, religious and philosophical activities were all broadly in accord'.[111] For Eliot the European high Middle Ages, with Thomas and subsequently Dante as their supreme embodiments, was the best expression so far of this ideal. So Maritain admirably suited his turn. Both men had the intellectual audacity needed to venture a philosophy and theology of history. The American historian of twentieth-century English Christian thought Adam Schwartz writes that these

> two modern critics claimed history as the poet's province in their time because of what they perceived to be the abdication by modernist historians of the responsibility to fuse the particular and the general, the matter and meaning of history into a coherent pattern.[112]

In effect, Maritain came to displace Charles Maurras, whose role in Eliot's outlook was of much longer standing, but whose veneration for the French seventeenth century – certainly a great age for the Catholic Church – was entirely detached from credal commitment of

---

[110] T. S. Eliot, 'The Modern Mind', art. cit., p. 137.

[111] P. Ackroyd, *T. S. Eliot*, op. cit., p. 155.

[112] A. Schwartz, 'Theologies of History in G. K. Chesterton's *The Everlasting Man* and in David Jones's *The Anathemata*', *Chesterton Review* XXIII. 1-2 (1997), pp. 65-82, and here at p. 65.

any kind.[113] Earlier, Eliot's anti-Romantic, anti-Liberal sentiments had combined to form his admiration both for the French Symbolist poets and Maurras' cultural politics.[114] He had been reading Maurras since 1908, struck in the first instance by the French analyst's 1905 work *L'Avenir de l'intelligence.* On Maurras' version of French history: after the Bourbons, French culture had endured a dictactorship of unrealistic literary ideas. Napoleon I sought to control ideas bureaucratically but only produced a false order. In the nineteenth century, the revolutionary ideal of fraternity led to nationalism while its concept of the primacy of the individual generated an anonymous individualistic society. Free intellectuals still existed but they were dependent on a market where opinion was shaped by the press and ultimately, behind the press, high finance. Maurras' monarchism derived not from a sacramental vision but from the conviction that the monarchical institution (and with it the nobility, Church and army) was in this situation a desirable countervailing force.

Maurras' influence on Eliot waned after Eliot's Baptism in 1927, but the – evidently programmatic – essay 'The Idea of a Literary Review', published in *Criterion* for 1926, shows him attempting to combine references to Maritain and Maurras. Nor was this an inherently improbable exercise since Maritain had

---

[113] For the contrasts as well as communalities between Maurras and the early Maritain, see P. Chenaux, *Entre Maurras et Maritain. Une génération intellectuelle catholique 1920-1930* (Paris 1999).

[114] E. Beer, *Thomas Stears Eliot und der Antiliberalismus des XX. Jahrhunderts* (Vienna 1983).

gravitated towards Maurras' movement, while eschewing Maurras' philosophy, until the Roman condemnation of *Action française* in 1928. That early phase of Eliot's Gallic interests was lastingly significant in the way it propelled Eliot towards the English 'Metaphysical' poets of the seventeenth century who, he believed, succeeded in combining disparate elements in experience in much the same way the Symbolist poets did later in France. David Jones, to whom I shall turn in a moment, had learned from Eliot when he commented approvingly on how the Metaphysicals had 'managed to wed widely separated ideas, and to make odd scraps of newly discovered data subserve immemorial themes'.[115] In a footnote Jones described this poetry helpfully, albeit in a somewhat idiosyncratic idiom of his own:

> counter-Renaissant, creaturely yet other-world-ordered, ecstatic yet technically severe and ingenious, concerned with conditions of the psyche, but its images very much of the soma; metaphysical, but not un-intrigued by the physics of the period; English, but well represented by names hardly English...[116]

Jones agreed with Eliot, then, on the paramount need for the re-integration of England's cultural life. But it was Eliot's sense of the *level of depth* at which such re-integration needed to happen that made him part company with Maurras' social philosophy the very name of which betrayed its debt to the atheistic thought of Comte: *positivisme organisateur*. As Eliot's

[115] D. Jones, 'The Preface to *The Anathemata*', in idem., *Epoch and Artist* (London 1959), pp. 107-138, and here at p. 114.
[116] Ibid., n. 1.

1931 ruminations on the previous year's 'Lambeth Conference' of the bishops of the Anglican Communion made clear, he now considered the 'real conflict' to be between theistic faith and atheistic 'faith': a division it was 'all for the best' to draw as sharply as can be. 'For any man who thinks clearly, as his Faith is so will his morals be.'[117] The catholicising tendency leading the Anglican bishops at that juncture to closer relations with the Eastern Orthodox churches would, he thought, tend to a greater stability than the present formal establishment of the national church since

> Christianity in spite of certain local appearances is not and cannot be within measurable time, 'official'. The world is trying [in England, q. v.] the experiment of attempting to form a civilized but non-Christian mentality. The experiment will fail, but we must be very patient in awaiting its collapse; meanwhile redeeming the time: so that the Faith may be preserved alive through the dark ages before us, to renew and rebuild civilization, and save the world from suicide.[118]

In a similar vein, he had once commented on the ethical writings of his Oxford research topic, the philosophy of the English Idealist F. H. Bradley:

> A system of ethics, if thorough, is explicitly or implicitly a system of theology, and to attempt to erect a complete theory of ethics without a religion is none the less to adopt some particular attitude towards religion.[119]

---

[117] T. S. Eliot, *Thoughts after Lambeth* (London 1931), p. 9.
[118] Ibid., p. 32.
[119] Idem., *Selected Essays*, op. cit., p. 416.

There is no doubt that in the inter-War years Eliot sometimes considered Fascism a lesser evil than Liberalism, but his traditionalism held him back from any real commitment to the radical Right. Fascism was Napoleonist. Unlike traditional monarchy, it was, he wrote in 1929, a 'doctrine of success'. So far from constituting an antidote to capitalism the feeling for dictators it encouraged was merely 'the consummation of the feeling newspapers teach us to have for Henry Ford'.[120] Eliot's basic conviction was that the wider frame of democracy had been destroyed, which was why giving the people what the people wanted could no longer be considered, when taken by itself, a sound or admirable maxim to follow. Was 'what the people wanted' good *in se*?

Eliot's *After Strange Gods*, his most controversial adventure in cultural politics, praised unified rooted culture, settled on the land and opposed to cosmopolitanism. (David Jones would later call this 'the actual land itself, its sites and its rooted communities and all that has hitherto afforded a connection, however fragmented and attenuated, with the foundational things.'[121]) Together with his conviction that to the degree possible a society should share a common religion, that explains his notorious – but frequently over-interpreted – remark about the undesirability of large numbers of free-thinking Jews. The words 'free-thinking' and 'large numbers' must be given their

[120] Idem., 'Mr Barnes and Mr Rowse', *Criterion*, July 1929, p. 689.
[121] D. Jones, 'Preface by the Author' in idem., *Epoch and Artist* (London 1959), pp. 11-18 and here at p. 16.

due weight. One might not unfairly compare a later liberal commentator remarking on the undesirability of permitting the entry into England of large numbers of militant Muslims, where again in all justice the qualifying terms would need to be suitably weighed. In *Notes towards the Definition of Culture* Eliot remarked on the desirability of 'close culture-contact between devout and practising Christians and devout and practising Jews', as distinct from that contact between Jews and Gentiles emancipated from their religious traditions which in the recent past has served to 'strengthen the illusion that there can be culture without religion'.[122]

Eliot's conviction that England needed an integrated moral, philosophical, religious and aesthetic existence finds expression in numerous asides, such as: 'We have the same respect for Blake's philosophy ... that we have for an ingenious piece of home-made furniture: we admire the man who has put it together out of the odds and ends about the house'.[123] When he adds that 'the concentration resulting from a framework of mythology and theology and philosophy is one of the reasons why Dante is a classic, and Blake only a poet of genius',[124] and that our national 'mythology' has suffered from both the suppression of ancient paganism and the divorce from Rome,[125] we find ourselves moving with this analytic Eliot via Christopher Dawson toward his fellow Modernist poet, David Jones. In the reconstructive –

[122] T. S. Eliot, *Notes towards the Definition of Culture*, op. cit., p. 70, n. 1.
[123] Idem., 'Blake', in *The Sacred Wood* (London 1920; 1960), p. 156.
[124] Ibid., p. 158.
[125] Ibid., p. 157.

rather than critical – mode of this thinking we look more with the Anglo-Catholic 'sociologists' who contributed to *Prospect for Christendom*, showing a concentration of mind and heart on the integral evangelical task extremely rare in modern English Christianity and no doubt to be explained in part by the sense of urgency which accompanied the last year of the Second World War. It was the first year of peace – but peace of what kind?[126]

David Jones

The transition from Eliot to Jones is easy. Eliot wrote:

> It would be no gain whatever for English culture, for the Welsh, Scots and Irish to become indistinguishable from Englishmen – what *would* happen of course, is that we should all become indistinguishable featureless 'Britons', at a lower level of culture than that of any of the separate regions. On the contrary, it is of great advantage for English culture to be constantly influenced from Scotland, Ireland and Wales ... We have not given enough attention to the ecology of cultures.[127]

And speaking of Welsh poets – and poets of Welsh extraction – writing in English Eliot declared, if the Welsh became less Welsh their poets would 'cease to have any contribution to make to English literature, beyond their individual genius'.[128] Eliot does not hesitate to call

[126] M. B. Reckitt (ed.), *Prospect for Christendom. Essays in Catholic Social Reconstruction* (London 1945).
[127] T. S. Eliot, *Notes towards the Definition of Culture*, op. cit., pp. 55, 58.
[128] Ibid., p. 57.

some version of this scenario 'calamitous'. It is hard to think it is not David Jones above all whom he has in mind.

In 1939 Jones wrote to René Hague, Eric Gill's son-in-law:

> I feel bewildered with the noise of contrary ideas and the infernal complexity of religion, sex, the structure of society, the arts and everything. All these chaps have bits of right ideas, and when you can see and sympathize with all the various apparently stark contradictory notions it is hard – hard enough to equate in one's own poor head, let alone explain.[129]

He was working at the time on the (never completed) *Book of Balaam's Ass* which uses the battlefield as a metaphor for contemporary civilization. The modern world is a babel of confused voices, a place where 'they don't give a bugger to … be without the holy city'.[130] In *The Dying Gaul*, moreover, Jones had this to say:

> Certainly men never more needed to contemplate form, they need all there is to remind them that all evidence to the contrary, the end of man is happiness. The 'parts that are united in one' in an artwork may be, for some, the most convincing analogy which they can get to in this world of the 'proportioned parts' of the heavenly city, to delight in which, religion says, is part of our redeemed destiny.[131]

[129] D. Jones, *Dai Greatcoat. A Self-Portrait of David Jones in his Letters*, ed. R. Hague (London 1980), p. 94.

[130] D. Jones, *The Roman Quarry*, eds H. Grisewood and R. Hague (London 1981), p. 190. (Only a fragment of the 'Book' was regarded by Jones as sufficiently publishable; it is incorporated in this work as 'Balaam's Ass'.)

[131] Idem., *The Dying Gaul*, ed. H. Grisewood (London 1978), p. 135.

Jones was emphatic – against all the idealisms, whether Left or Right, of the 1930s – that the heavenly city belongs with humanity's *redeemed* destiny and is not realizable in social life on earth.[132] In the Preface to the 1937 War epic *In Parenthesis*, citing the Tudor prosist Sir John Mandeville, he declares the peace of the City of God 'fer beyonde' history. And yet he considered that *some* providential design could be discovered not least in the 'matter of Britain' to which the vast canvas of his second book-length poem, *The Anathemata,* is devoted. Even though he found the form-making characteristic of art – but pervasively displayed by man the creative animal – to be a more hopeful place to seek for anticipations of the peace that passes all understanding, he certainly did not despise what Dawson called, in a phrase which perhaps caught the young J. R. R. Tolkien's eye, 'the middle earth of life and history'.[133]

What Jones most profoundly held – and *The Anathemata* is the witness to this – was that the prehistorical and historical events which moulded ancient Britain (and therefore England) are best recalled in the context of sacred time; the time of the Mass whose unfolding gives the poem its basic context and even structure. That is why he can hold that 'these events

[132] P. Deane, 'David Jones: Poet of the Thirties', *The Chesterton Review* XXIII. 1-2 (1997), pp. 147-155. Deane contrasts Jones' attitude here with that of Dawson in his 1931 *Christianity and the New Age* , and indeed, the entire series *Essays in Order* , the principal English Catholic contribution to the ideological ferment of the period of which Dawson, along with T. F. Burns of *The Tablet*, was general editor. Note Dawson's enthusiastic introduction to Carl Schmitt's *The Necessity of Politics* (London 1931).

[133] C. Dawson, *Beyond Politics* (London 1939), p. 121.

both exist in their own time, "long, long, long before" and are present "here and now"'.[134] But in terms of its wider content, the poem traces, in Jeremy Hooker's words

> a tragic tension between the degeneration of Western culture and the eternal revelation that shaped its development when the Word became flesh and hence operative in historical time. Now, though what the signs signify is eternally valid their temporal validity is under assault.[135]

This sets the basic conditions on which the poem's reflections proceed.

Whether as poet or artist Jones had two chief themes: recollection (in biblical, patristic, liturgical as well as philosophical Greek this reads 'anamnesis'), and sacrament or efficacious sign. If *In Parenthesis* is a personal anamnesis of the First World War, the *Anathemata* represent a more universal recollection, concerned – focally but not exclusively (there are wider concentric circles: Europe, Earth, the cosmos itself) – with the memory of Britain and the different peoples who have had a part in its making. As Jones put it in the preface:

> What is this writing about? I answer that it is about one's own 'thing', which *res* is unavoidably part and parcel of the Western Christian *res*, as inherited by a person whose perceptions are totally conditioned and limited by and dependent upon his being indigenous

---

[134] J. Hooker, 'On *The Anathemata*', *The Anglo-Welsh Review* 22. 50 (1973), pp. 31-43, and here at p. 34.
[135] Ibid., p. 36.

> to this island. In this it is necessarily insular; within which insularity there are the further conditionings contingent upon his being a Londoner, of Welsh and English parentage, of Protestant upbringing, of Catholic subscription.[136]

Jones' vision is, for the 'realm', highly inclusive, then, and yet he does not blur the uniqueness of the one act of God in Christ. Instead, he shows us something of the extent to which the uniqueness is *inclusive not exclusive*, revealing how all things relate to the one central point of redemption and healing. As the Jones scholar Thomas Dilworth puts it, the Eucharist is the 'nucleus' of the book's 'orbiting images', because it is 'the great Symbol, synonymous with time's central redemptive event'.[137]

> The exploration of time in *The Anathemata* extends back into prehistoric fore-time, but only during the three millennia of western history does a spiralling shape emerge. This shape is that of a continual metamorphosis which formally evokes and extends through history the geological and evolutionary mutations of fore-time. During the historical millennia, culture-phases rhyme to form a pattern centring at the time of Christ. In this respect David Jones shapes his synthesis of Spengler and Frazer to traditional patristic historiography. ... Christ [is] at its temporal centre ...[138]

The difficulty for Jones was not so much theological as historical. In the conditions of modern Britain, where

[136] D. Jones, 'The Preface to *The Anathemata*', in idem., *Epoch and Artist*, op. cit., pp. 108-109.
[137] T. Dilworth, *The Shape of Meaning in the Poetry of David Jones* (Toronto 1988), p. 154.
[138] Ibid., p. 183.

technology is not only a material instrument but the set of a mind, how can we find that realm which must be 'actually loved and known'?

> Normally we should not have far to seek: the flowers for the muse's garland would be gathered from the ancestral burial-mound – always and inevitably fertile ground, yielding perennial and familiar blossoms, watered and, maybe, potted, perhaps 'improved', by ourselves. It becomes more difficult when the bulldozers have all but obliterated the mounds, when all that is left of the potting-sheds are the disused hypocausts, and when where was this site and were these foci there is *terra informis*.[139]

Nor, it may be added, can the situation be improved by the addition of theme-parks, which are not likely to be artefacts capable of fructifying the poetic understanding of memory. But the difficulty of executing the project is precisely why a poet of genius was needed. Of course, it is one man's journey down the 'history-paths' – Jones does not eschew those 'living, dying, or dead traditions in which one has oneself participated or heard of with one's own ears from one's own parents or near relatives or immediate forebears' – but the sheer range of monuments he draws into the 'sprawl' of his 'pattern' creates confidence in him.[140] After listing an enormous variety of sources from Geraldus Cambrensis and Anselm of Canterbury through John Stow, author of the 1598 *Survey of London*, and Herbert of Cherbury to

[139] D. Jones, 'The Preface to *The Anathemata*', in idem., *Epoch and Artist*, op. cit., p. 121.
[140] Ibid., pp. 127, 135.

Kipling, Jones adds a more foundational reference to

> the basic things: the early mixed racial deposits, the myth (mythus) that is specifically of this Island, and the Christian Liturgy, and the Canon of Scripture, and the Classical deposits … a great complex of influences and interactions which have conditioned us all.

Jones linked together art and sacrement, broadly conceived. As to 'sacrament', the poet is, in a term borrowed from the Dominican aesthetician Thomas Gilby, a 'hunter of forms', *venator formarum.*[141] Jones was supremely a lover of signs. But he was also obliged to face the problem of their validity at a time when cultural and religious tradition was exceedingly fragmented. Visual as well as literary artist, Jones celebrated the cosmos by his craft: his frontispiece to a Welsh translation of Ecclesiastes shows the Christian artist seated in his cell, poised over a picture of a fish, and surrounded by animals, birds, flowers and the tools of his trade. Since the beginning of man's history, so Jones wrote in an essay found in the collection *Epoch and Artist*,

> this creature juxtaposed marks on surfaces not merely with utile, but with significant intent; that is to say a 'representing', a 'showing again under other forms', an 'effective recalling of something' was intended … We have ample evidence to show us that palaeolithic man, whatever else he was, and whatever his ancestors were, was a sacramental animal.[142]

[141] Ibid., p. 116.
[142] D. Jones, 'Art and Sacrament', in *Epoch and Artist*, op. cit., pp. 143-179, and here at p. 155.

It was the source of his quasi-despair with modern living conditions that 'the technocracy in which we live, and which conditions us all, tends, in all sorts of contexts and at every level, to draw away from this sign-world'.[143] Jones emphasised the unity of the abstract and the representational in art. As the paradigm of artistic making the Eucharistic Gifts are an abstract art *par excellence*: nothing further from representational realism could be conceived. It is the abstract quality in a picture which gives it its proper 'being', making it a thing in its own right and not just the impression of some other thing.[144] But at the same time this makes possible discernment of the – representational – relation between the reality or object that is the point of departure and the final product that is the picture. For Jones, however, this formal statement of the nature of art had nothing at all to do with the paring down of poetic matter to the minimum (judges of the Tate Gallery's 'Turner Prize' please note!). Quite the contrary, in fact, as the above account of *The Anathemata* may suggest.

> The arts abhor any loppings off of meanings or emptyings out, any lessening of the totality of connotation, any loss of recession and thickness through.[145]

---

[143] Idem., 'Preface by the Author', in ibid., p. 13.
[144] Idem., 'Art and Sacrament', in ibid., pp. 170-171. See also his letter 'Abstract Art' in the same volume, where he remarks, 'Those of us whose work no one, I imagine, would call "abstract", know, nevertheless, that it is an abstract *quality*, however hidden or devious, which determines the real worth of any work', p. 265.
[145] Idem., 'The Preface to *The Anathemata*', in *Epoch and Artist*, op. cit., p. 120.

For Jones, then, any adequate account of 'The Matter of Britain' had to be mythopoeic in character: one where salient features of the historical culture, identified with an eye at once poetic and metaphysical, are translated into appropriately mythic form. As he wrote:

> To conserve, to develop, to bring together, to make significant for the present what the past holds, without dilution or any deleting, but rather by understanding and transubstantiating the material, this is the function of genuine myth, neither pedantic nor popularising, not indifferent to scholarship, not antiquarian, but saying always, 'Of these thou hast given me I have lost none'.[146]

Christopher Dawson

The common bond of Eliot and Jones – poetic technique apart – was surely Christopher Dawson. The preface to the first edition of *Notes* names Dawson along with V. A. Demant (of the Christendom sociologists) as the two most pervasive hidden presences of the book. Jones rarely failed to disclose his debt to Dawson, not least in the footnotes to *The Anathemata*. Already in 1936, the preface to *In Parenthesis* invites readers to accept the mingled references to 'Englishry' and 'Welshry' of the poem for a Dawsonian reason: 'it is the conservatism and loyalty to lost causes of Western Britain that has

---

[146] Idem., 'The Myth of Arthur', in ibid., pp. 212-259 and here at p. 243. The Arthur myth is extremely important to Jones as the '*Iliad-Aeneid* of the Celtic-Germano-Latin Christian medieval West': thus his 'The Arthurian Legend', in ibid., pp. 202-211, and here at p. 204.

given our national traditions its distinctive character'.[147] (So the mediaevals were right to make Arthur and not Alfred, say, the central figure of the island's heroic legend.) But the debt is far more wide-ranging than such occasional, albeit interesting, convergences.

On the basis of developments in early twentieth-century anthropology and ethnology, Dawson held that

> we are witnessing the rise of a new science which will study man's past not as an inorganic mass of isolated events but as the manifestation of the growth and mutual interaction of living cultural wholes.[148]

There has become possible, he argued, a 'general vision of the whole past of our civilization', which will show, among other things, its more than national unity. (In this work, published ten years after the end of one World War and ten years before the start of another one, the future peace of Europe was clearly a dominant preoccupation, as it would be virtually throughout Dawson's *oeuvre*.)

Like Eliot who, as already noted, drew on his work, Dawson devoted a good deal of effort to the definition of culture. Essentially, he thought, a culture is 'a common way of life', [149] but whereas three elements that go toward its make-up – race, geography and economics – can be paralleled in the animal kingdom, where they appear

---

[147] Dawson was reviewing R. G. Collingwood and J. N.L. Myres, *Roman Britain and the English Settlements* in *The Tablet* for 5 December 1936.
[148] C. Dawson, *The Age of the Gods. A Study in the Origins of Culture in Prehistorical Europe and the Ancient East* (London 1928), p. v.
[149] Ibid., p. xiii.

as genetics, environment and function, in the case of humanity we must also add *thought*, a psychological factor. And that is key, since:

> It is this factor which renders possible the acquisition of a growing capital of social tradition, so that the gains of one generation can be transmitted to the next, and the discoveries or new ideas of an individual can become the common property of the whole society. In this way a human culture is able to modify itself more rapidly and adapt itself more successfully to a new environment by an inheritance of acquired characteristics, such as does not seem to exist in the purely biological law of development which governs animal species.[150]

Though a culture is a community of blood, place and work as well as thought, any attempt to lay exclusive weight on one of these produces a racial, geographical or economic determinism quite as implausible as 'false theories of abstract intellectual progress'. Progress, where it exists, is irregular and spasmodic, an inference of a simplyifying kind from manifold heterogeneous changes.

For Dawson, the texture of culture is in notable part determined by the past, for each past condition expresses itself in the 'life-impulses and life-concepts of a society'. But to this must be added the roles of *reason and religion*. He names first reason, whose frequent capitalisation in Dawson's text is no doubt explained by the citation that follows:

> Reason is itself a creative power which is ever organising the raw material of life and sensible experience into

[150] Ibid., p. xiv.

> the ordered cosmos of an intelligible world – a world which is not a mere subjective image but corresponds in a certain measure to the objective reality.[151]

The bracketing of religion with reason is illumined when Dawson goes on:

> Every religion embodies an attitude to life and a conception of reality, and any change in these brings with it a change in the whole character of culture, as we see in the case of the transformation of ancient civilisation by Christianity, or the transformation of the society of Pagan Arabia by Islam. Thus the prophet and the religious reformer, in whom a new view of life – a new *revelation* – becomes explicit, is perhaps the greatest of all agents of social change, even though he is himself the product of social causes and the vehicle of an ancient cultural tradition.[152]

By the time he wrote *Religion and the Rise of Western Culture* in 1950, Dawson was convinced that the chief anthropological problem facing us is 'the problem of religion and culture', and this on the ground that their intricate inter-relation governs the union between the 'social way of life' and the 'spiritual beliefs and values which are accepted by society as the ultimate laws of life and the ultimate standards of individual and social behaviour'.[153] Dawson feared that increasing academic specialization might create a vacuum in awareness to be filled only bureaucratically – by official education, information, publicity which functioned, deliberately

[151] Ibid., p. xix.

[152] Ibid., p. xx.

[153] Idem., *Religion and the Rise of Western Culture* (London 1950), p. 4.

or not, as an ideological screen.

> It would be a strange fatality if the great revolution by which Western man has subdued nature to his purposes should end in the loss of his own spiritual freedom, but this might well happen if an increasing technical control of the state over the life and thought of its members should coincide with a qualitative decline in the standards of our culture.[154]

Though a faith serves the same social purpose as an ideology, it also

> looks beyond the world of man and his works; it introduces man to a higher and more universal range of reality than the finite and temporal world to which the state and the economic order belong. And thereby it introduces into human life an element of spiritual freedom which may have a creative and transforming influence on man's social culture and historical destiny as well as on his inner personal experience.[155]

Pointing out that his generation (having lived through two World Wars and witnessed the rise of Bolshevism and Fascism) has been obliged to see how fragile is the barrier between civilization and destruction, Dawson declares it should be so much the better placed to grasp the 'vital function of religion both as a principle of continuity and conservation and as the source of a new spiritual life'.[156] Alas, the modern media, by stressing the current and immediate, induce short memory span. That is why Dawson's potential English readers in the

[154] Ibid., p. 6.
[155] Ibid., p. 7.
[156] Ibid., p. 19.

early twenty-first century are not necessarily aware (they may have read journalism by Richard Dawkins) that secular ideologies, great power interests, and ethnic conflicts wrought infinitely greater havoc in the preceding century than did any religious movement.

G. K. Chesterton

Jones belongs to High Modernity, Chesterton was a Late Victorian. Yet they enjoy a commonality which goes far beyond the (interesting) coincidence that both were received into the Catholic Church – Jones a year before Chesterton – by the same priest, Father John O'Connor of St Cuthbert's, Bradford, the original of Chesterton's clerical detective, 'Father Brown'. [157] Not least, Jones's 'theology of history' – as found in *The Anathemata* especially – is extraordinarily akin to that of G. K. Chesterton, notably in the latter's *The Everlasting Man*, the principal theological writing of his Catholic (as distinct from Anglo-Catholic) period.[158]

> [A]n examination of these two works reveals that Chesterton and Jones share a theology of history arising from their Catholicism, a hermeneutic centered on Christ and His Crucifixion, the pivotal person and event in history to them. This belief provides a focal point to which they relate all other persons, events, rites, and myths. In making these connections, the two writers simultaneously defend the values of tradition and continuity while stressing

[157] W. Blissett, 'David Jones and the Chesterbelloc', *Chesterton Review* XXXIII. 1-2 (1997), pp. 27-55, and here at p. 28.
[158] G. K. Chesterton, *The Everlasting Man* (London 1925).

> the qualitative difference made by Christ … [T]heir common contention that all things rhyme in Christ leads them to assert the unique abilities of Christianity to synthesize reason and imagination as well as to limit the scope of historical subjects while expanding their substance.[159]

A passionate union of imagination and intellectuality is the hallmark of Chesterton's greatest and best known work, the masterpiece of his Anglo-Catholic period, *Orthodoxy*.[160] This book is still the best apologia for the faith for English readers who have never known it – or, having once known it, have forgotten what it is. The problem Chesterton sets himself is to show how vital for us it is to feel astonished at the world and yet at home in it – a very interesting way of introducing the questions of metaphysics. Chesterton describes his discovery that Christianity – which he defines as the Apostles' Creed and the moral conduct that flows from it – is the perfect grounding for this feeling: first, it educates us in that feeling, helps us towards a mature experience of it in its twofold structure (astonishment at the world, and being at home in it); secondly, it legitimises the feeling by setting out doctrines that enable us to see how the feeling is metaphysically fitting, how it fits with reality at large.

Of course, 'feeling' is an inadequate term here. It's a question of our basic not only emotional but also thinking, registering, analysing, understanding attitude to the world, and in both senses – affective and cognitive

[159] A. Schwartz, 'Theologies of History', art. cit., p. 66.

[160] G. K. Chesterton, *Orthodoxy* (London 1908; many times reprinted, e.g. London 1996).

– our basic response to life. To be able to approach the world as a mixture of the familiar and the unfamiliar, as a world where we feel welcome, at home, and yet which elicits from us wonder – astonishment – is, says Chesterton, the basis of an active and imaginative life.

It helps to see what Chesterton means here by considering alternative life-styles. For example, a drug-stupified existence, where people seek support for the self through chemical substances, is not likely to be active though, as Aldous Huxley reported on LSD, it could be imaginative! Again, a functional, utilitarian type of life, as in the welfare materialism which is the main ideological form of current English society, is not likely to be imaginative though it may well be highly active. Failing to combine active and imaginative, neither is the good life as Western man has classically understood it.

Chesterton's efforts to dig out the fundamental presuppositions of treating the world as home yet astonishing – in other words, his efforts to disengage an appropriate philosophy for living – led him to make a remarkable discovery. When putting the finishing touches to his philosophy he suddenly realized it was indistinguishable from that implied by the orthodoxy of the Church. Hence the book's title. Here was more wonderment, since the Church was the last place Chesterton expected to look. The background to his book was the so-called Edwardian cultural crisis, induced by the effect on the English elite of such developments as Marxianism, Darwinism, Nietzschean nihilism, Shaw's atheistic Fabian Socialism, and H. G.

Wells's scientific positivism.[161] It was a major chapter in the story of the progressive secularisation of British society, the origins of which go back to the middle of the nineteenth century. So, as Chesterton said, he felt like an English navigator who, thinking he was in the South Seas, landed on a strange shore and armed to the teeth and communicating with the natives by signs, planted the Union Jack on a grotesque and barbarous temple, only to discover it was the Brighton Pavilion. It is no use saying orthodoxy is incredible because it belongs to another age. What a man can believe depends on his philosophy not his century.

For the most part, Chesterton does not attack the then current – and still potent – alternative philosophies in terms of the specific tenets of each. Rather, he tries to identify the false presuppositions they have in common, presuppositions that can be known to be false because, if followed up or followed through, they would make impossible that combined being astonished at the world and being at home in it he has already found to be essential to healthy living.

In different ways, the alternative philosophies combine logical completeness with spiritual contraction, and in this, Chesterton argues, they mirror the madman in whom just this combination can be observed. Typically, they make people doubtful about the aims of personal existence, which is paralysing, whereas what we *should* be doubtful about is only the quality of our efforts to reach those aims, which is galvanising. The

[161] J. D. Coates, *Chesterton and the Edwardian Cultural Crisis* (Hull 1984).

systematic scepticism they induce about fundamental values makes their criticism of what remains of religious authority resemble the folly of a man who attacks the police force without ever having heard of burglars.

By contrast, the philosophy of orthodoxy maintains that in four key propositions listed by Chesterton:

- the world does not explain itself;
- there is something personal in it as in a work of art;
- despite its odd design its purpose is beautiful;
- the proper form of thanks to it is some kind of humility and restraint (as in gratitude for Burgundy by not drinking too much of it).

In Chesterton's cosmology in *Orthodoxy*, the world is a wild and startling place which might have been quite different but is quite delightful. Before this wildness and delight, we should be modest and, as he puts it, 'submit to the queerest limitations' (such as monogamy) of 'so queer a kindness' (such as sex).

Crucial to the mixture of astonishment and familiarity with which we should dwell in the world is wonder at the gratuitousness of things existing as they do. They could so easily have been other. Trees growing red apples are as extraordinary as trees growing golden candelabra or stripey tigers. That is:

- we can't say that a world of any sort *had to* exist;
- much less can we say that the world had to take the form of this kind of world, a world based on carbon rather than, say, silicon;
- and still less that this kind of world had to develop as precisely *this* ecology of species that we have.

Words like 'law' and 'necessity' are inappropriate in this context because, as Chesterton writes in a philosophically sophisticated formulation, they 'assume an inner synthesis we do not possess'.

All this is explicable if, as the Creed claims, the world was made as if a work of art by a Creator who 'threw it off': that is, separated it off from himself in the act of creation and subsequently gave it over to human devices. Nature is not our mother – those who worship her as such may be innocent and amiable in the morning but are likely to be cruel by evening. No, nature is our sister. Nature, resourceful but dangerous, is inhabited by man as a race turned toward the good but defectively so, through original sin. We recall that for Chesterton, Christianity is not only the Apostles' Creed, it is also the moral conduct that issues from it. Belief in original sin is one of the unattractive parts of Christianity that make possible what are among the most attractive virtues in it. Accepting the doctrine of original sin enables us to pity the beggar and laugh at the prince. As the book makes clear, we cannot stop short with the philosophy and not move on to the doctrine, since the only sane view of the natural is to be found in the supernatural.

For Chesterton, human history – and behind that the fundamental place of man in nature – is inexplicable unless heaven has been twice on earth: once to set up in the human animal the image of God, and the second time to become incarnate in the Founder of Christianity. Where is the evidence for the Creator's involvement at these two key points, the human creation in the divine image and the entry into humanity of God as Jesus Christ? This is the topic of the last sections of *Orthodoxy*.

The evidence, Chesterton claims, is there to be surveyed precisely in those areas which critiques of Christianity highlight. Once investigated, these are what reveal the faith's wider rational foundations by reversing the thrust of the criticism offered. Such critics act despite themselves as midwives for Christian apologetics. Thus for instance on the claim that the human species is in fact only a variety of the animal kingdom Chesterton writes:

> That man and brute are like is, in a sense, a truism; but that being so like they should then be so unsanely unlike, that is the shock and the enigma. That an ape has hands is far less interesting to the philosopher than the fact that having hands he does next to nothing with them; does not play knuckle-bones or the violin; does not carve marble or carve mutton. People talk of barbaric architecture and debased art. But elephants do not build colossal temples of ivory even in a rococo style; camels do not paint even bad pictures, though equipped with the material of many camel's hair brushes. Certain modern dreamers say that ants and bees have a society superior to ours. They have, indeed, a civilisation; but that very truth only reminds us that it is an inferior civilisation. Who ever found an ant-hill decorated with the status of celebrated ants? Who has seen a bee-hive carved with the images of gorgeous queens of old? No; the chasm between man and other creatures may have a natural explanation, but it is a chasm. We talk of wild animals; but man is the only wild animal. It is man that has broken out. All

> other animals are tame animals; following the rugged respectability of the tribe or type. All other animals are domestic animals; man alone is ever undomestic, either as a profligate or a monk. So that this first superficial reason for materialism is, if anything, a reason for its opposite; it is exactly where biology leaves off that all religion begins.[162]

Chesterton caps these points by a line of argument which is, so far as I know, exclusive to himself. Certain ways of combining what could be regarded as mutually exclusive behaviours such as mercy and due severity, chastity and procreativity, are part and parcel of what most people would regard as desirable ethical common sense. Such moral syntheses derive, so Chesterton maintains, from 'the moral atmosphere of the Incarnation'. They would not have become apparent to us without the Incarnation. They are combinations, not amalgams, of virtues which the mysteries of Christianity enable us to keep distinct and so observe in their integrity. They are as distinct as the red and white on the Cross of St George, whereas, once deprived of their essential reference point in the Incarnation, life, teaching and example of Jesus and his Paschal mystery, they would flow disastrously into each other as a definitely undesirable not red-and-white but pink.

How does Chesterton end? He ends with the characteristically Chestertonian concept and virtue of joy. A philosophy adequate to healthy happy living demands that joy be, as he writes, 'something gigantic' and sadness 'something special and small'. The orthodoxy of the Church can alone satisfy this demand. And this

[162] G. K. Chesterton, *Orthodoxy* (London 1996), pp. 213-214.

surely is because, though Chesterton doesn't spell this out, after the Ascension of the Lamb who was slain and the deification of our humanity in him, the sins of the world are now anomalies, anachronisms. They no longer indicate the destiny of man, the future of the world.

What does indicate it? Asking the question brings us to Tolkien.

J. R. R. Tolkien

As is (fairly) well known, one of Tolkien's chief aims in writing *The Lord of the Rings* was to supply the English with a mythology all their own – granted that, as Eliot regretfully noted, their pagan past had not provided much of consequence in this direction. There is little doubt that Tolkien deliberately related his material to pre-existing mediaeval and English traditions, using an ancient narrative technique of weaving together parallel stories in a fashion which perhaps recalls the Anglo-Celtic art of interlace which so fascinated David Jones. Equally venerable is the fashion in which Tolkien hints at other stories only implicit in *The Lord of the Rings* but rendered explicit, often, in his more highly developed mythology, *The Silmarillion.*

The 'mythology' Tolkien provided in *The Lord of the Rings* itself takes the form of fantasy laid out as epic. It has been proposed that fantasy became in twentieth-century English literature, if not only there, the dominant genre because it was the appropriate way to respond to the traumas the century held.[163] *The Lord of*

[163] T. A. Shippey, *J. R. R. Tolkien. Author of the Century* (London 2000);

the Rings certainly addresses the issue of evil, its origin and status, and evil had been remarkably re-focussed for England from 1914 to 1945. Its other major themes include cultural relativity; the corruptions of language; and life without the support of (supernatural) revelation – for Tolkien was seeking, in the name of a 'good' paganism, a mediating standpoint between Christian and non-Christian in his audience. Its specifically Christian conviction is that ultimately all will be turned to good – but it is not so turned yet, not by a long chalk. Tom Bombadil, that rather truncated 'Green Man' figure, sings of the final 'eucatastrophe' – Tolkien's term for the ultimate turn to the good – when he banishes the 'barrow wight' who has sought to enclose the engaging hobbit Meriadoc in his icy hold, banishes him to 'where gates stand for ever shut, till the world is mended'.[164] One of Tolkien's chief animating convictions was that one should fight for the good even if, humanly speaking, one will be defeated. That much of the work was produced in 1940 is probably not irrelevant. The way he appeals to inherited traditions to confirm the will to face seemingly insuperable enemies might not unfairly be called Churchillian.

'Eucatastrophe' plays a major part in what Tolkien was by no means unhappy to call 'fairy stories'. As he put it in his essay 'On Fairy Stories':

> Fairy-stories were plainly not primarily concerned

---

see the (even) fuller earlier study by the same author, *The Road to Middle Earth* (London 1982).

[164] J. R. R. Tolkien, *The Lord of the Rings* (London 1954-5; as one volume, 1968; 2005), p. 142.

> with possibility, but with desirability. If they awakened *desire*, satisfying it while often whetting it unbearably, they succeeded.[165]

Such desire may be for different goods (Tolkien mentions, for instance, two such contrasting goals as insight into the 'depths of space and time', on the one hand, and 'communion with other living things' on the other). But the most decisive good for which desire can be awakened is knowledge of reality as generative of joy. Within the limits of the world of 'faery' that 'knowledge' is granted only for a fictional secondary creation. But that is not the whole story. As Tolkien explains:

> [I]n the 'eucatastrophe' we see in a brief vision that the answer may be greater – it may be a far-off gleam or echo of *evangelium* in the real world.[166]

The word 'gospel' (*evangelium*) can be invoked here because, thinks Tolkien, the Gospels themselves have as their principal content 'a story of a larger kind which embraces all the essence of fairy stories'. As he defends this unusual statement:

> They contain many marvels – peculiarly artistic [since 'the Art is here in the story itself rather than in the telling, for the Author of the story was not the evangelists'], beautiful and moving: 'mythical' in their perfect, self-contained significance; and among the marvels is the greatest and most complete conceivable eucatastrophe.[167]

There is, however, a difference not only of scale or

165 Idem., 'On Fairy-Stories' in idem., *Tree and Leaf* (London 1964), p. 39.
166 Ibid., p. 62.
167 Ibid.

intensity but also of kind. *This* story has entered the primary world. It has become history. The Resurrection of Christ is the 'eucatastrophe' of the Incarnation which itself is the 'eucatastrophe' of human history at large. The 'Christian joy', what Tolkien terms 'the *Gloria*', would here be infinite if our own capacity for experiencing it were not finite. '[T]his story is supreme; and it is true. Art has been verified ... Legend and history have met and fused.'[168] And not the least good thing to emerge from it is the hallowing of the human making of romances and 'fairy-tales', all narratives, even when fantastic, that have a happy ending.

For the Tolkien of 'On Fairy-Stories' we live in an age of 'improved means to deteriorated ends'.[169] It is an age of technically proficient reductionism. As has been well said:

> It remains a supreme, but understandable irony that Tolkien's 'illusive' universe, after a decade of limited fame, took its first dramatic rise to the stratospheric heights of mass popularity at the very moment in the mid 1960s when the Church was in the throes of making its cultic worship more 'relevant' by shearing off from it the ordered, hieratic dimension of sacred play. For many orphaned souls, asphyxiated by the banality of modern life, Tolkien was opening a window to transcendence that was just then being peremptorily drawn shut by the officious matrons of this liturgical revolution.[170]

168 Ibid., p. 63.

169 Ibid.

170 M. Sebanc, 'J. R. R. Tolkien: Lover of the Logos', *Communio* 20. 1 (1993), pp. 84-106, and here at p. 88.

We continue to need mythopoeisis, the creation of secondary worlds that will throw light on a primary world now known to be not only a divinely created cosmos but one predestined to be summed up in Jesus Christ. The ordered thaumaturgic field of play that is *The Lord of the Rings* may be potent enough to open up the true dimensions of a God-related, God-dependent, cosmos with an implicit Christological ethos thanks to the importance there of humility and *little* things, as well as to the theme of unexpected triumph through suffering endured. As Tolkien was aware, this opening to transcendence could not come about without stirring the moral imagination.

Our next figure, Hilaire Belloc, would have said the same about worthwhile engagement with history.

Hilaire Belloc

Jones's technique as bardic interpreter of 'The Realm' has a likeness to Hilaire Belloc's in the latter's 1908 collection of historical monologues, *The Eye-Witness*. (We note especially Belloc's concern for topography.) Belloc has been called the wreck of a great historian. Impatient – unlike Jones, who had learned from Dawson – of the travail of careful reading and comparison of sources, he was nonetheless possessed of acute perceptiveness about past epochs as well as narrative power in re-presenting turns of events.

But it is as social analyst, notably in *The Servile State*, that he most merits attention. In modern Collectivism Belloc found only 'the riveting of Capitalism more securely round the body of the State'.[171] The ancient

[171] H. Belloc, *The Servile State* (London and Edinburgh 1912), p. 181.

liberties, secured by bonds of covenanted duty but also enabling the spontaneous pursuit of corporate goals, would be replaced, he thought, by a new conformity in which people only imagine they are free.[172] (That is represented a hundred years later by the domination of the consumer-cum-celebrity culture.) More constructively, in his Distributivist economics, which owed much to contemporary papal social teaching, Belloc maintained that, as far as possible, the means of production ('Property') should be owned by the family unit, trading with other family units under the umbrella of guilds to control not merely quality but fairness of pricing to both producer and consumer. Elements of that same theory are under re-construction by Catholic economic theorists today.[173]

Distributism came to little or nothing because its timing was unfortunate. Belloc's *Essay on the Restoration of Property* was written in 1928, the year Henry Ford laid down the first modern production line in Detroit. Profitable growth markets until well after World War II were all for mass produced items. In agriculture the new availability of tractors plus cheap oil led to the mechanised exploitation of large scale fields, driving many off the land. Most industries became dominated by oligopolies through mergers and takeovers. But now technology and areas of profitability have changed. Large integrated corporations are considered dinosaurs, and are being re-engineered to contract out many

[172] Ibid., p. 183.
[173] J. Médaille, *The Vocation of Business. Social Justice in the Marketplace* (New York and London 2007).

functions to independent consultants. In Germany it is small companies that do best in mechanical engineering, while information technology thrives on freelance computer programmers. A new breed of educated craftsmen seems to be emerging, to meet the sense of disgust at the blandness of machine production. Such small producers need a mutual association guaranteeing standards and providing guidance in the efficient use of finance and equipment. The Middle Ages would have called that 'guilds'.

At least in sections of society, trends of opinion began to form in the 1960s that were remarkably reminiscent of the (largely unnoticed) 'Distributivist' Catholic social apologetics of the early decades of the twentieth century. Marquand calls it:

> a shift of mood and aspiration – a growing suspicion of hierarchy, bureaucracy and complexity; a longing for the small-scale and the familiar; a growing demand for wider participation in decision-making; in some quarters, at any rate, a new disdain for the economism of the post-war period and even a new hostility to the pursuit of economic growth.[174]

Some at least of the cultural, technological and industrial mutations of recent years favour this. There is a turn to small-batch production and flexible specialisation, to which the appropriate political economy may be 'yeoman democracy'.[175] Perhaps it would not be possible to introduce widely a practice of this kind without opting

---

[174] D. Marquand, *The Unprincipled Society*, op. cit., p. 48.
[175] M. J. Piore and C. Sabel, *The Second Industrial Divide: Possibilities for Prosperity* (New York 1984).

out of the world free-trading system. But organizations like in the United States the Capital Ownership Group and Jeff Gates' Shared Capitalism Institute have at least a family resemblance to Distributivism. Agriculture has a pivotal role in a Distributist economy: many people can be employed in a physically and spiritually helpful way in procuring that food that is the primary need of man. Bodies like the (American) Agrarian Foundation and the Homesteading Movement seek to renew a way of life that is close to nature, concerned with primary production and a form of labour where family members can collaborate. Such a way of life may well have a future, even in England. After all, the English love affair with England is most intensely a love of the husbanding of the English landscape.[176]

[176] See the classic W. G. Hoskins, *The Making of the English Landscape* (London 1955); D. Matless, *Landscape and Englishness* (London 1998).

Chapter 5

INTEGRAL EVANGELISATION

With some notion of the 'needs of the nation' and the contribution of the culture critics or, better, 'sages', Catholic and Anglo-Catholic, to their illumination, we are now better placed to take up the challenge of the opening chapter of this book by considering what is involved in evangelisation that is really *integral* in character.

Introduction

T. S. Eliot wrote:

> When we consider the quality of the integration required for the full cultivation of the spiritual life, we must keep in mind the possibility of grace and the exemplars of sanctity in order not to sink into despair. And when we consider the problem of evangelisation, of the development of a Christian society, we have reason to quail.[177]

The question of how the Church is to evangelise is no new one, and a principled answer would be worth stating in any age. The fact is, however, that urgency is added to the question by what are often seen as the peculiar difficulties of presenting the faith in the current cultural climate, at any rate at the European end of the North Atlantic civilization.[178]

---

[177] T. S. Eliot, *Notes towards the Definition of Culture*, op. cit., p. 32.
[178] R. Rémond, *Religion et société en Europe: la sécularisation aux XIXe et XXe siècles* (Paris 2001).

> The society in which we live no longer seems to resound to the rhythms of divine grace, it has lost the religious habits of the heart and can no longer speak the language of religious tradition.[179]

It is of course true that the rolling wave of secularisation in Western Europe is much more of a gentle trickle in the United States,[180] and yet these two great human solidarities have enough in common – one thinks of the various secularising judgments handed down by the American Supreme Court since 1947[181] – for complacency anywhere to be out of place. Perhaps the beginning of the twenty-first century is as good a time as any to look around and take stock of both the challenges and the resources the Catholic tradition can bring to them. And this is so not least because the sort of society and culture we have now may be with us in much the same form for quite some time.

Just what sort of society and culture might that of the imminent future be? It has been suggested that the condition of things we are entering could best be described as a 'steady-state post-industrial society'.[182] It

[179] A. White, O.P., 'Between Exile and Redemption: a View of the Catholic Church in England', *New Blackfriars* 85. 995 (2004), pp. 5-16 and here at p. 5.

[180] A lapse of twenty years is hardly sufficient to explain the contrast between on the one hand C. Brown, *The Death of Christian Britain: Understanding Secularisation 1800-2000*, (London 2000) and E. Norman, *Secularisation*, op. cit. and on the other R. J. Neuhaus (ed.), *Unsecular America* (Grand Rapids, Mich., 1986). For the problems of the principal Catholic (demographic) donor-nation to the Church in the United States, see D. Vincent Twomey, S.V.D., *The End of Irish Catholicism?* (Dublin 2003).

[181] R. Hittinger, *The First Grace*, op. cit., pp. 163-182.

[182] I owe this phrase – and the idea – to the privately based Cambridge

is true that without the charism of prophecy futurology is no well-grounded pursuit. But we cannot help noting that the structure of matter allows of exploration and exploitation only as finite as itself. The time will come, and perhaps is closer than we think, when the limits of technology-induced change are in effect reached, such that no fresh breakthroughs of a kind liable to transform dramatically human lives at large are likely, by this route, to occur. The 'unlikelihood' involved is not simply that of indefinite new advances in knowledge. It is also a question of the disinclination of contemporary consumerist societies to fund massive technological projects of uncertain benefit, projects that of their nature would dominate, if not monopolize, disposable revenue. The phrase 'the Middle Ages with computers' could sum up, albeit journalistically, the consequent notion of a technologically competent stasis. If there be any truth in this, it has the advantage that, should we be able to develop the right evangelical strategies now, they will stand us in good stead for years to come.

However this be, what is certain is how in various ways the state of things in the post-industrial West bears little relation to the historic Middle Ages of Christendom. We only have to think of such peculiarly modern phenomena as, for example, the dominance of commercial image in advertising and the media exploitation of personality cult, encouraging people as these do to value themselves and others for reasons disconnected from the virtues. Or again, there is

---

analyst, William Hutton (conversation of 18 February, 2004).

the *anomie* whereby the young arrive in the state of adulthood having neither internalized obligations, nor acquired a sense of living under authority – so great has been the reduction in moral force of the family, extended or nuclear, and the weakening of deference to civic tradition and the State. In the past, such deference has been open to abuse. Yet this danger must be balanced against the implications of a generalized unwillingness, outside Islamic polities at least, either to die for or in any very costing way to live for civilization-based ideals.

These two factors alone – the dominance of marketable image and the prevailing *anomie* – might suffice to explain a third difference in expectation that seems a distinctive malaise of societies of our kind. And this is the replacement of neighbourliness by indifference or neglect as people restrict their benevolence to those with whom for the moment they consider themselves in love, and/or those of whose economic good will they stand in need – employers, landlords and the like. Emblematic is the way common friendly courtesies are tending to vanish from public thoroughfares and public transport, as also the reduced participation in local or national politics noted as a general trend in the European democracies. The disorientation bred in many by social and geographical mobility, with their tendency to wither lasting loyalty to firm or locality, adds to a general sense of the lack of meaning and order in life. To this the response in many cases will be a search for immediate gratification and the achieving of temporary oblivion through drink, drugs or sex.

The wounds sustained in the culture-wars of Western modernity could be summed up, then, as: the draining away of human substance (as presentation becomes all), the severance of human roots (as the self becomes unanchored), and the fracturing of human bonds (as individual aggrandizement – dignified as the quest for 'fulfillment' – becomes ever more relentless). Mercifully, considerable numbers of people resist these trends. But the determination so to do is starting to look really rather heroic. And these particular wounds make even less probable the recovery of the patient from that universal post-Fall human sickness which declares itself to us in the seven deadly sins whose blood-lines run through every age. The disorder of the vices is even harder to deal with when entire societies, through lack of substance, roots and bonds, lose their sense of what might be the rightful ordering of the human world.

This makes it the more pressing that we should bring to bear on common life and personal life the healing and elevating resources of divine revelation, and the wisdom its marriage with human prudence has effected in the Catholic tradition. I believe that evangelisation – at all times, but with special urgency in the present conjuncture – should be carried out as 'integral evangelisation'. By this I understand an evangelisation which addresses all the dimensions of the person-in-society that Christian wisdom can help to flourish. This will mean treating divine revelation as a resource that can correct present errors, redress current vices and unmask the ambient ugliness, while still revering it for what in itself it is. That qualifying clause is important. Revelation is not merely a salve for our sicknesses. It is also an invitation to deification in the most wonderful epiphany of goodness, truth and beauty humanity can ever know. The Catholic faith is not another ideology. It cannot to be reduced to an instrument for the amelioration of culture. In evangelisation we must not stress cultural utility at the expense of the divine mysteries themselves. This was the temptation of Catholics involved in the early twentieth-century movement *L'Action française*. As Maritain saw in the nick of time, the spiritual must have the primacy. What the Church offers above all is food for the spirit and everlasting life with God. Authentic Christianity, and therefore authentic evangelisation, is not about us, it is about God. And so, as the Pastoral Constitution of the Second Vatican Council on the Church in the Modern World puts it:

> If anyone wishes to devote himself to the ministry of God's word, let him use the ways and means proper to the Gospel, which differ in many respects from those obtaining in the earthly city.[183]

On the other hand, as the Irish social commentator Desmond Fennell has pointed out, 'savvy' – his term for the prudent circumspection that scans the environment and takes everything into account – can further acceptance of the Gospel, and that in two ways. In his words:

> When the recipients are well-disposed, it evokes gratitude towards the evangeliser for a gift received, and consequently a greater trustful openness to his

[183] *Gaudium et spes*, 76.

> message's Gospel core. When the recipients are ill-disposed, it disconcerts them by its perceptible but unwelcome truth, reduces their public standing (if they have such) as definers of the situation, and consequently lessens their ability to offer confident opposition to the Church's teaching and to build support for this.[184]

Evidently, integral evangelisation is so large a topic that it can only be justified as the subject of a chapter (I have already confessed the 'monumental' character of the project this essay has in mind) if we accept the postulate of classical German philosophy that the true is the whole. To render it more manageable, I propose to break it down into three elements: intellectual, mystical, institutional. These are the categories in which the Anglo-German philosopher, the Baron Friedrich von Hügel (strictly, a Scoto-German, or, as he put it, 'half Scotch'), identified the principal elements of the Catholic religion in the opening chapter of his great two-volume investigation, *The Mystical Element of Religion as Studied in Saint Catherine of Genoa and her Friends*, published in London and New York in 1908.[185] The classification is not simply original but issues from the doctrinal tradition. Von Hügel based it on John Henry Newman's account of the three offices of Christ and his Church – prophetic, and thus intellectual; priestly,

[184] D. Fennell, *Savvy and the Preaching of the Gospel. A Response to Vincent Twomey's 'The End of Irish Catholicism'* (Dublin 2003), p. 4.

[185] F. von Hügel, *The Mystical Element of Religion as studied in Saint Catherine of Genoa and her Friends* (London and New York 1923, 2nd edition), pp. 50-82. For the writing of this work, see J. J. Kelly, *Baron Friedrich von Hügel's Philosophy of Religion* (Leuven 1983), pp. 73-100.

and thus mystical, and kingly, and thus institutional.[186] Newman's version – as with everything in Newman, far from standard or manualistic, is found in the 'Preface' he composed for a work of his Oxford period when he reissued it in 1877, this time as a Catholic, under the title *The Via Media of the Anglican Church.* I shall take the three elements in the order in which I have given them: first intellectual; secondly, mystical; thirdly, institutional, and ask in turn what issues they raise and materials they offer for 'integral evangelisation'.

The intellectual element

I begin with the intellectual element not least because in the tradition of thought of St Thomas Aquinas, the seat of the vision of God, though prepared by the loving will, is found in the mind. As Newman realized in his thoughtful retrospect on the Evangelicalism of his youth and early manhood, a religion of the sentiments alone is not only dangerously inadequate when squalls of feeling arise in the storms of life. There is also the problem that it cannot do justice to the way Christianity has an all-embracing 'Idea', the divine revelation with, at its center, the Incarnation of the Word. The Anglo-Catholic writer Dorothy L. Sayers wrote in 1947:

> It is hopeless to offer Christianity as a vaguely idealistic

[186] I leave aside the question of the influence of William James' 1897 essay 'Reflex Action and Theism' on the concrete way von Hügel applied his tripartite scheme to the genetic development of the individual who, beginning from sense impressions, moves through reflection to the discharge of the will in action. This is not pertinent to my concern here with the *corporate* Church as the bearer of evangelisation.

> aspiration of a simple and consoling kind; it is, on the contrary, a hard, tough, exacting, and complex doctrine, steeped in a drastic and uncompromising realism.[187]

Consequently, it is of the first importance to evangelisation that the minds of the Church's members be not only alert to contemporary culture but also well-stocked with maturely reflected and apologetically honed dogmatic truth. A Church that retains some power of moral uplift through its ceremonies and ministrations will make no evangelical headway in a high culture – and every high culture also permeates the broad culture given time – if in the meanwhile it has lost the intellectual argument.

Here the Church must set out forthrightly to recover lost ground. Unfortunately, many of the institutions which ought to be flagships, taking the lead in presenting, in the words of St Peter, the reasons for the faith that is in us,[188] have suffered shipwreck through secularization. Where it is too late to reclaim them, we should support initiatives to replace the services they once provided, even if at first these cannot replicate the material level of the lost facilities. The Church needs to devote renewed attention to apologetics, taking advantage in the English-speaking world of the new school of apologists flourishing in the contemporary United States. Where the information media are hostile, we can bypass their hidden or not so hidden agenda by creating alternative forums for instruction and public

[187] D. L. Sayers, *Creed or Chaos?* (London 1947), p. 28.

[188] Cf. I Peter 3: 15.

debate. In this perspective, might the Church do more to encourage Catholic professionals to see themselves as members of a Catholic intelligentsia with a special mission to society? That would require of them, of course, a capacity to articulate the faith. But this is one important form of achieving maturity in it. Above all, the Church must make it a priority to educate young people thoroughly and persuasively in its Creed.[189]

At the service of evangelisation we have the inestimable advantage of our sapiential tradition of philosophy, a tradition which derives from meditation on the Scriptures in the light of the wisdom welling up from ancient pagan springs. It was by a singular dispensation of Providence that the Hellenes managed to transmit with comparatively few distortions the voices of creation, and such crackling as there was on their receivers the witness of biblical revelation permits us to edit out. I like the idea of the American Orthodox priest Patrick Henry Reardon that the missions of the Son and the Spirit are what give us the orientation we need in philosophical discernment. The Father sent the Son in our flesh to validate yet transform the external empirical, historical order. This is the Word who for the First Letter of St John was manifested, whom the witnesses heard, saw and handled.[190] The Father sent the Spirit into our hearts – for Scripture the seat of understanding – to validate yet transform the internal order of knowing and certitude. This is the Spirit

[189] I take these desiderata from A. White, O.P., 'Between Exile and Redemption', art. cit., p. 14.
[190] I John 1: 1-3.

who, so the First Letter of St Paul to the Corinthians declares, is 'from God that we might know the things freely given us by God' – and know them, as the same apostle's First Letter to the Thessalonians insists, 'with complete certainty, *plērophoria pollē*'.[191] In the light of the economies of Son and Spirit we should have a serene trust both in the reliability of the empirical order and in the powers of the human mind really to know.[192] We should not fall into the trap indicated by the Anglican cleric and wit Sydney Smith when he reported on the negative results of philosophical enquiry in the century of his birth:

> Bishop Berkeley destroyed this world in one volume octavo; and nothing remained, after his time, but mind; which experienced a similar fate from the hand of Mr Hume in 1739.[193]

We by contrast have to hand a Christian philosophy that combines trust in the order of the senses with a confidence in the powers of mind. It bears the name of Thomas Aquinas, and its capacity to serve the Gospel is not yet exhausted. In Reardon's words:

> To know the truth is to have one's mind shaped by real form, *rei forma*, … to have one's mind contoured by the shape of being.[194]

Knowledge, accordingly, is a communion (*cognitio*

[191] I Corinthians 2: 13; I Thessalonians 1: 5.

[192] P. H. Reardon, 'Communion and Division: the Structure of Knowledge', *Touchstone. A Journal of Mere Christianity* 16. 6 (2003), pp. 85-92, passim.

[193] S. Smith, *Sketches of Moral Philosophy*, Introduction.

[194] P. H. Reardon, 'Communion and Division', art. cit., p. 90.

derives from *co-* as well as *gnosco*) in which we become one with the truth. Such a philosophy can act as a scourer to flush out of us the modern pseudo-spirituality that in the name of religion would replace determinate beliefs by an experiential, expressive quest for body, mind and self, or similar formulations. It is an antidote to that misunderstanding whereby, as has been said,

> modern people do not expect religion to constitute a structure of doctrine, but to furnish a kind of personal screen on which they can project sympathetic images devised by themselves.[195]

Now the varieties of theology which have found a place in the Catholic tradition are so many attempts to explore that communion of knowledge in the highest form known to humankind. And this is the covenant communion of life and understanding established with us by the gracious divine initiative through the saving revelation made in Jesus Christ. I would like to see a synthetic convergence of these theologies, a pooling of their resources in the service of the Church's common faith. We should be working towards a greater degree of unity in Catholic theological culture, on the basis of Scripture read in Tradition, and so with appropriate attention to the Fathers and the Liturgies, the Councils and the saints as well as the distinctive contributions of mediaeval and modern divines. That is a major desideratum if we are to practise evangelisation and catechesis on the foundation of a manifestly self-identical faith. The Creed is recited in the singular, *Credo* [not 'credimus'] *in*

[195] E. Norman, *Secularisation*, op. cit., p. 21.

unum Deum because it is confessed *in persona Ecclesiae*, in the 'person' of the one Church. And thus all attempts to expound the Creed, theology's essential task, should give primacy to unity not plurality, though a bounded plurality of different – but not contradictory – emphases and foci is not excluded.

In a University context, we are sometimes tempted to think that eliding or bracketing the supernatural component of Catholic theology is the only way to commend it to the academy. I am unconvinced of this, and not just for the reason that in Catholic Christianity 'the supernatural' is no mere building-block but, rather, what supplies the architecture for the structure as a whole. Drawing attention to the richness and complexity yet coherence and quasi-unity of our theology's conceptual treasure is likely to gain it more sincere respect, and the only kind worth ultimately having. (That, after all, is how sympathetic scholars not themselves Buddhists consider Buddhology or, though not Hindus, the achievements of Indian philosophy.) Showing how our tradition provides generous nourishment for thought is another form of *praeparatio evangelica*.

The mystical element

At its highest, such thought concerns the relations the Infinite has established with the finite. This brings us to the second of von Hügel's 'elements', the *mystical* element in evangelisation.

The mystical element in the Christian life concerns the heart of personal salvation – namely, sanctification and its perfection: *théōsis*, 'deification'. Through the mystical element in our religion we are able in evangelisation to present the Church as a school of prayer. 'We are able' here in two senses. We are able so to present the Church both because, objectively, the Church in fact is such a school, and because, subjectively, the mystical furnishes us with the personal spiritual energy that is necessary if we are to bear witness to her so being. This mystical element can be regarded as, in an important sense, formed by the element we have just been considering – by the intellectual, by doctrine. The mind of the Church, found in the monuments of Tradition as a whole and rendered where need be magisterially, gives us the key for interpreting what St Paul calls our 'reasonable worship'.[196] And in its turn, as we shall see, the mystical element is to impact on the institutional whose ethos it prevents from becoming, among other things, rationalist or bureaucratic.

In Catholicism, the heart of the mystical is provided by the Liturgy which forms the template for prayer of all kinds, and shapes the ethos of the Church as a wondrous sacral home preparing us for the life of eternity – just as our domestic home is meant to prepare us for the life of time. Through the Liturgy our personal entry into the mysteries of the divine saving plan for us takes place – once for all in Holy Baptism, reiteratively in the rest of liturgical prayer with the Mass at its heart. The Constitution on the Sacred Liturgy of the Second Vatican Council reminds us:

---

[196] Romans 12: 1.

> Every liturgical celebration, because it is an action of Christ the Priest and of his Body, which is the Church, is a sacred action surpassing all others. No other action of the Church can equal its efficacy by the same title and to the same degree.

And that text continues:

> In the earthly liturgy we take part in a foretaste of that heavenly liturgy which is celebrated in the Holy City of Jerusalem toward which we journey as pilgrims, where Christ is sitting at the right hand of God, minister of the holy of holies and of the true tabernacle.[197]

The liturgical celebration of the Lord's 'cross-over', his Pasch, is what has given authentically Christian mystical spirituality its most enduring features. These include its sense of: the transience of the world and the glory of God; the fleeting nature of fortune and the mercy of God; the inevitability of tragedy and the victory of God; the centrality of humility and the cognate humility of God. It is through such spirituality that the Liturgy forms our imaginations – a pretty crucial part of becoming evangelists and getting others to grasp the inwardness of Catholic Christianity. When the Liturgy fails to fulfil this function we must beware, bearing in mind Newman's prediction that where belief falters it is above all because 'the imagination is against us'.[198]

The Liturgy should impact on civil society through public sacral times and spaces. Hence the importance of feast days kept as general holidays or what the mediaeval

[197] *Sacrosanctum Concilium* 7-8.

[198] C. S. Dessain et al. (eds), *The Letters and Diaries of John Henry Newman*, Volume XXX (Oxford 1977), p. 102.

English called 'fair days' – and in countries where Catholics, or Christians more widely, form a significant proportion of the population the dominant rhetoric of multi-culturalism could well be exploited to demand civic recognition of such festivals. Hence too the role of pilgrimages and processions, and of church buildings conceived not merely as houses of the community but houses of God, where a rich patrimony of sacral music, art and architecture can assist the performance of rites and devotions that are themselves condensed forms of the mystical. All of these sensuous signs enable Christian mysticism to travel across the boundary between the inner and the outer world. And this is appropriate because distinctively Christian mysticism has its origin in the synthesis of inner and outer that is the Word incarnate in his mysteries: Christ's inner consciousness filled with the treasures of divine wisdom, his outward bearing full of grace and truth.[199]

The ability of the Liturgy to sustain the mystical element in the Church is, I believe, crucial to the Church's survival as an agency of evangelisation. In the powerful yet soft secularising totalitarianism of distinctively modern culture, our greatest enemy is what an English Church historian has described as the Church's 'own internal secularisation' which, when it occurs, does so through the 'voluntary and largely unconscious' adoption of the 'ideas and practices' of seemingly 'benign adversaries'.[200] The ability of the Liturgy to generate Christian mysticism is our most

[199] Cf. Colossians 2: 3; John 1: 14.
[200] E. Norman, *Secularisation*, op. cit., p. ix.

powerful antidote to what Edward Norman calls 'the insistence of church leaders themselves on representing secular enthusiasm for humanity as core Christianity'.[201] Though this statement is made chiefly in regard to Anglicanism, it would be foolish to underestimate the extent to which it can apply to Catholicism also – and with it the prospect of an increasing evacuation of internal substance. A Church which travels this road is insufficiently distinct from its environment to be the focus of passionate loyalty. Its faithful, saddened and demoralized, gradually desert it. In the end it suffers social death by its own hand. That is why the re-enchantment of the Liturgy and the full restoration of its sacral character are so vital an issue for us.

The appeal to the mystical element in our religion will always have evangelical force. As von Hügel saw, and here I cite from one of his most distinguished interpreters:

> Man's continual unrest and dissatisfaction with all purely immanent realities springs from the fact that he experiences this as immanent only in relation and in contrast to something other and permanent, transcending the mere process of this world.[202]

In von Hügel's own words, it is because human beings

> have the dim, inarticulate sense of what the Abiding means that the mere slush of change is so sickening.[203]

---

[201] Ibid.

[202] J. J. Kelly, *Baron Friedrich von Hügel's Philosophy of Religion*, op. cit., p. 166.

[203] *Baron Friedrich von Hügel: Selected Letters 1896-1924*, edited by B. Holland

That heartsickness is something which through the Liturgy, when celebrated and experienced *sub specie aeternitatis*, evangelisation can address. Von Hügel was clear that, to return to the interpreter, J. J. Kelly,

> even the most exclusively mystical soul always requires some contact with finite, contingent spatio-temporal reality and with society since the mystical sense is evoked only on such occasions.[204]

Above all, Christians who receive in Holy Baptism a call to contemplation must through a properly incarnational mysticism live simultaneously on the two levels, time and eternity, not separating these since they are 'polar aspects of the same experience'.[205] This brings us inevitably to our third and final 'element', the institutional.

The institutional element

The institutional element in the Church is concerned with polity and policy. We may take polity first.

Polity is the institutional element in the Church considered *ad intra*, in terms of the Church's own life and mission. Institutional Christianity is impossible without Christian institutions. The fundamental Christian institutions are those that follow from the basic patterning of the Church in a sacred order or 'hierarchy': the bishops, assisted by the deacons; the presbyters or ministerial priests of the second grade; the monks and other ascetics (what modern Catholicism

---

(London 1927), p. 364.

[204] J. J. Kelly, *Baron Friedrich von Hügel's Philosophy of Religion*, op. cit., p. 172.

[205] Ibid.

calls 'Religious'); and the laity. On the health of this entire *hierarchia*, and not on that of any one order within it, turns the health of the whole Church. No expansion of the apostolic activity of the laity can compensate in a local church for the disappearance of the consecrated life, nor is it any consolation, if membership of the priesthood is haemorrhaging, to be told that vocations to the episcopate are never lacking.

Each of these orders, or primary institutions, has, corporately or in collaboration, responsibility for other – we can call them 'secondary' – institutions. Such secondary institutions range from episcopal Conferences and parishes through schools, health-care institutions, and societies and movements of numerous specialised kinds, to the Christian household or, where there is the generation and nurture of new human beings, the Catholic family. From a sociological standpoint, the Catholic family is also an institution, and a crucial one for a Church that grows by birth and infant Baptism as well as by conversion and adult initiation. The family has been a tremendously diverse institution in human history and what it stands for depends on the values it proposes to transmit. In our case that will mean of course the plenary Gospel.

There can be no fully efficacious evangelisation unless the ethos of this institutional life draws people. And this for the reason that this varied common life, the life of the household of faith, is until the Lord's Parousia all we have to show when we say to enquirers, echoing the words of Jesus to the earliest candidates for discipleship, 'Come and see'.[206] The institutional life of the Church will not assist but rather hamper evangelisation unless it has at all levels a corporate spiritual atmosphere that is detectible – at any rate, with a modicum of sympathy. And this is so not only in a presbytery but at an administrator's desk or in a scholar's study, or with the family gathered round the dining table (which of course is where, rather than in easy chairs facing a television set, they ought to be). Some contemporary Eastern Orthodox theologians like to call this common institutional life and action of the Church 'the Liturgy after the Liturgy'. This formula makes the important point that every expression of the Church as polity should be treated as a continuation of the Liturgy, of the Church's appropriation of her life received from the Trinity, in Christ, through the nuptial mystery of the Cross. The range of attitudes, of postures of mind and heart, which the Liturgy calls forth from us ought to be perpetuated to the degree possible and in the manner pertinent throughout the day. Our religion is concerned with worship, service and right personal conduct. For us, efficiency only ever means spiritual efficacy – though that should not be taken as an excuse for failing to answer letters!

By 'policy', as distinct from 'polity', I understand the institutional element in the Church considered *ad extra* – as facing out to the wider civil commonwealth beyond and encompassing the ecclesial society. This distinction *ad intra*, *ad extra* is a necessary one, even if we were in the (hypothetically possible) position of a

[206] John 1: 39.

society all of whose members are Catholic Christians. Even then the forms of civil society, as well as the State itself, would continue to have their own rationale and thus legitimate autonomy. (So it was with the *regnum*, as distinct from *sacerdotium*, of the Middle Ages.) This is the more obvious if, as is in modern conditions a good deal likelier, Catholic Christians are in the position of a minority in civil society or, indeed, the position of a *mere* majority – the word 'mere' there indicating an important principle democracy is tempted to truncate. In speaking to civil society, or the State, the Church uses what some would call its 'secular voice'. Personally, to avoid the ever-ambiguous language of secularity, I prefer to call this the tone in which, tutored by the saving revelation, the Church expresses in accents not heard since before the Fall, the voice of creation.

The modern democratic State is ambivalent about the Church, no matter what the political colour of the government in power – not that such colours now represent much more than shades of grey. That State has emerged from the more modest – if sometimes in limited respects authoritarian – constitutional State of the world before the First World War and the succeeding Depression. Its characteristics are to encourage the equality and self-determination of individuals while setting no limits to the magnification of its own ruling power. In order to achieve the former goals, the latter is indispensable as means. Huge areas of social exchange are to become subject to State regulation if the currently approved practices and attitudes are to reign. Implied is the dissolution of any traditional authority – whether of clergy, parents or local communities – that might impede the State's work of emancipating individuals along these lines. Such emancipation takes the form of inculcating, where once the norms of Christian morality held sway, new rules more appropriate to the citizen as free consumer of commodities not excluding sex. Increasingly this is a neo-pagan confessional-secular State with as its quasi-religion the 'politically correct' moralism of the day.

In such a context, what might the institutional element in evangelisation mean? Evangelisation of the State power means its confrontation with the abiding objectivity of the natural moral law, itself an expression of the divine Wisdom, and the measure of all positive law on earth. Human beings govern – whether as law-makers or legislators, law-enforcers or rulers, or law-adjudicators or judges – only by participation in a higher law, by sharing in the care of divine providence for the common good, as by reference to moral truth people build characters that can fit them for life everlasting. No State is excused from the worship of God and obedience to a moral law both integral to that worship and the only stable foundation for human rights.[207] Woe to that State which accepts the seduction of the serpent in the

[207] In the words of Orestes Brownson, the natural law 'is not a law founded or prescribed by nature, but the law for the moral government of nature, under which all moral natures are placed by the Author of nature as supreme law-giver. The law of nature is God's law; and whatever rights it founds or are held from it are his rights, and ours only because they are his.' Cited in R. Hittinger, *The First Grace*, op. cit., p. xxv.

garden, 'Ye shall be as gods' and seeks to establish the 'natural measures of good and evil'.[208]

The State's recognition of a higher norm – something implied in different ways in the founding documents of the American Republic and the Coronation ritual of English monarchs, prepares the way for an acknowledgement of Christian revelation, of which the coronation ceremony indeed is a quasi-sacramental expression. This brings us to the distinctively Christian aspect in the evangelisation of civil society.

What is specifically Christian in our message to the wider civil society is the message of theocentric humanism. The religion of the Incarnation, just because it is *so* theocentric, being lived for the Father's glory, also knows the price God has placed on man. The divine prizing of humanity for which the Son died and the Spirit was poured out is the sign of God's faithfulness to his original creative intent: human beings are made in his image and likeness. There is then a real evangelical significance in the interventions the Church makes on behalf of the image of God in man, so often obscured and even despoiled. The Church cannot remain silent if legislators become libertarians, underwriting a radical individualism rooted in almost unrestricted optionality. Such libertarianism has little in common with the political Liberalism of earlier generations which was founded on a common moral consensus. Here the litmus-test must be the issue of abortion, since unless life, once created, survives it can inherit no other

208 Ibid., p. 55.

right. Here the natural law inscribed in the human conscience finds transfigured expression by the light of the Crucifixion, in the Catholic defence of the weakest, the most vulnerable: the unborn. Pro-life activity is also Gospelling.

Policy must be directed evangelically to public officers, but also to the world of work, the proper domain of the Catholic laity. We know that the lay vocation has what the Second Vatican Council calls an *indoles saecularis,*[209] an *indoles* or 'innate character' that is *saecularis,* which has nothing to do with the English 'secularism' or even 'secularity' but simply means 'of its time'.[210] The home of the lay vocation is in the world of this age, the creation groaning with travail until now – unlike the priesthood and monastic life which of their very nature look primarily to the eternal, to the abiding Age to Come. *Gaudium et spes* invites the laity to 'impress the divine law on the affairs of the earthly city'[211] – in other words, to evangelise culture. Sayers, from whom I have already quoted, placed at the heart of the lay vocation in this context the issue of worthwhile work. 'All good and creative handling of the material universe is holy and beautiful', she wrote.[212] And that notion of a holy tradition of working was at the centre of the social philosophy of various English Dominicans, including their Tertiaries, now called 'Lay Dominicans',

[209] *Lumen Gentium*, 31.

[210] *The Oxford English Dictionary (on Historical Sources)*, III (Oxford 1983), p. 1926.

[211] *Gaudium et spes*, 43.

[212] D. L. Sayers, *Creed or Chaos?*, op cit., p. 35.

in the first half of the twentieth century. It is a weightier and more central issue for the evangelisation of culture than at first it seems. In retrospect, we can better discern the nature of the intervention these writers were making on behalf of a society expressive of the Gospel. They were not against technology – labour-saving devices of various kinds – as such, even though the threat to traditions of craftsmanship worried them. Their protest was against what the American legal philosopher Russell Hittinger has called 'the machine insofar as it promises an activity superior to the human act'.[213] The ensemble of technologies with which we live generates cultural habits that are or can be profoundly inimical to the Gospel and indeed to the humanity called to perfection in the natural as well as supernatural orders. When sufficiently sophisticated, serving an alliance of commerce and the managerial class, tools become not simple human instruments but – what they should never be – the measure of the human world. Thus for example, the invention of the contraceptive pill has had profound effects on the heterosexual family; while the invention of *in vitro* technologies is making possible the homosexual family now arriving. 'Savvy' in discerning the effects of such developments, and finding ways of enhancing the ability to counter them, if only in the mode of oracular warning used by the Hebrew prophets, belongs with integral evangelisation too.

[213] R. Hittinger, *The First Grace*, op. cit., p. 264. Hittinger explains his indebtedness to the cultural historian Christopher Dawson, who in various of his writings declared the post-Liberal 'planned society' had as its distinctive feature the aim of reproducing culture by technology.

Society benefits from civil recognition of the public significance of the Church. A Church does not need to be formally established at law. But a society moves the more towards illumination the better it can see in the Church's values something of the identity and tradition it itself wishes to enjoy and transmit. In England we have a decayed Christian State which has surrendered its concern with the spiritual nurture of citizens, while failing to find any alternative body of principles whose application could adequately define the moral authority of the State. The resultant void is an evangelical problem. It is also, however, an evangelical opportunity.

Conclusion

It might not unreasonably be thought a fatal weakness of this chapter on evangelisation to have attempted so much, albeit organised by reference to a skeleton scheme, indebted to von Hügel, which, I hope, has saved my jellyfish from being totally invertebrate. But, as in the opening chapter, my contention is precisely that only a co-ordinated advance on a whole host of issues simultaneously really meets the need of the hour. One of the problems of the modern era is the way the various constitutive elements of culture do not fit into any meaningful totality. The sovereign territories of each field of endeavour do not converge on any horizon of meaning. Evangelisation means offering a spiritual symbiosis of the sort that alone can enable a community to survive as an organic unity. Such a symbiosis is only possible – this is the message of Sacred

Scripture if anything is – when a community submits to a transcendent *telos*, an overarching goal or end received, and received gladly, from beyond itself.[214]

The demands of evangelisation are, then, not only analysis of what may be comprised in the intellectual, mystical and institutional elements of revelation as carried in the Church's tradition. They also extend to the synthesis of what we have found by analysis, and its projection as a comprehensive vision of the faith as culture-creating as well as soul-care. The Kingdom of God is, certainly, a destiny for persons, but not persons as atomically considered. It is a destiny for persons as inhabiting an entire ecology of salvation.

Evangelisation so conceived also requires, like evangelisation in any form, the gift of hope. At the present time, global business is said to be suffering from a mood of 'irrational pessimism' of which the most obvious symptom is the mesmeric hold on managers of 'risk aversion'. Of course some industries have been hit by real problems: information technology and airlines spring to mind. But the problem runs deeper in that risk aversion can become a permanent mind-set and mode of operation almost independent of what takes place in the world. In some places, an unwillingness to take chances has become 'factored into' the everyday course of doing business. The issue of corporate reputation becomes dominant. Procedures for self-regulation take up increasing time and energy. Many initiatives are left to one side since a possible negative outcome is so

[214] L. Dupré, *Metaphysics and Culture* (Milwaukee 1994), p. 15.

feared. Far more energy is devoted to retaining existing customers than to creating new markets with bold new products. Business, like the wider society, over-reacts to developments such as terrorism that pose no huge threat to the great majority of people. It reacts to the world in a jittery, anxious fashion. Economic analysts have identified a new phenomenon: the ability to 'talk oneself into a recession'.

I do not think that anyone even moderately familiar with states of mind in the Catholic Church in Western Europe and North America will find it too difficult to draw an instructive parallel. An English bishop has called a consultation of clergy and people 'Forward and Outward'. This is probably due to the belief that, left to themselves, their motto will be 'Backward and Inward'. As we have seen, 'backward and inward' in a non-pejorative sense of those words have a real place among us. Without continual reference to the apostolic Tradition as displayed and deployed in the different generations of the Church's life, her intellectual, liturgical and institutional life will be shallow indeed. Retrospection in the Holy Spirit is a necessity for us. We of all people cannot be what W. B. Yeats called 'unremembering hearts and heads',[215] and must be on guard against the attempt by pundits to deconstruct the moral authority of a Christian past now judged wanting by often crude and ill-informed argumentation soaked in secular moralism. Likewise, without the personal interior appropriation of that tradition in a way that

[215] W. B. Yeats, *Under Ben Bulben*, V.

ultimately has to be called mystical – without, namely, personal mystagogical catechesis by the divine Master – none of the rest is anything worth for us. Inwardness by the Holy Spirit is a necessity for us. And yet the bishop is right: without the motion of 'forward and outward', without the missionary extension of the Church and the spread of her salvifically civilising influence we have simply not heard – or worse, if heard then not obeyed – the Great Commission with which St Matthew, the most ecclesial of all Gospels, ends.[216] That Commission is the ending with which we, as disciples, must over and again begin.

[216] Matthew 28: 18-20.

Overall Conclusion

This book has considered the call of Catholic Christians to re-convert to the faith of the Gospel the Dowry of Mary: the England that is her 'especial dower' – in the words of the 'mandate' that King Richard II desired Archbishop Thomas Arundel of Canterbury to issue at Lambeth in 1399.[217] In the opening chapter, we saw how this call is being neglected, despite its congruence with the missionary renewal sought by the Second Vatican Council, and that it is not as unrealistic as people say – not at any rate, in one main aspect: what I termed the apostolically favourable 'bi-polarity' of English Catholicism. In any case, resuming the mission of the conversion of England is unavoidable by us, being as it is the translation into the here and now of the dominical Great Commission.

Next, in chapter 2, we reminded ourselves, very schematically, of some distinguishing features of 'Albion'. I began from the Lindisfarne Gospel-book, since that artefact is an icon of the Christian faith as nation-making for the peoples of this island. I suggested that key to the identity of English national life was the interplay of four institutions: law, monarchy, parliament and Church. These I regard as inter-related (more or

[217] For a brief account, see M. Elvins, *Old Catholic England*, op. cit., pp. 1-4.

less happily at different epochs) within an implicit 'social covenant' that is typical of a baptised nation. The Reformation rupture disturbed the equilibrium of these elements, but voices in Anglicanism from the early Stuarts to the Oxford Movement allowed much of the 'Catholic' view of Church and society still to be heard. I pointed out that England never had 'a 1789': unlike in France, there has been no 'Great Revolution' to sweep Christendom away.[218]

In Chapter 3, we found the 'needs of the nation' to consist first and foremost in a recovery of common purpose, specifically of the kind a properly functioning culture should be able spontaneously to nurture, just as it has in the Christian past. In the baptismal context, a social covenant furnishes a combination of obligations and liberties that is expressive of duties as well as rights. Civil society is a *societas societarum*, a 'society of societies' – families, associations and the like, each authority-bearing at its own level – of which the State provides the overall governmental form. If the members of society are to accept exigent ethical demands, and not succumb to consumerist hedonism, the State must preserve its openness to revelation, where a greater truth, goodness and beauty come with divine sanction. The venture of 'Christian Democracy' *à la Maritain*, seeking to preserve Christian 'values' but without public reference to any transcendent source of truth, did not succeed. The

[218] That is why Professor John Milbank of Nottingham can dedicate his extraordinarily influential book *Theology and Social Theory: Beyond Secular Reason* (Oxford 1990) not only to his wife but also to the 'remnants of Christendom'.

authority of the State should not be invoked so as to substitute for moral and spiritual culture. Rather, such authority should guard it (as in the ritual drama of the 1953 Coronation rite), assisting a culture appropriate to the 'people of the English' to flourish. This it cannot do by appeal to opinion polls or support groups; it requires, we noted, the delineation of an objective common good. I ended by entering a due caveat about the distinctive space needed by individual persons – something easily imperilled by the over-politicisation of modern life.

From the kind of culture envisaged, a range of virtues desirable both for persons and communities can proceed. Much of English literature, and the public moralists who have influenced the poets, explores what those virtues – moral and intellectual – are. So in Chapter 4, I recommended a number of twentieth-century writers, Anglo-Catholic and Catholic, who sought to constitute an overall English Christian culture suited both to this island and the Catholic faith. At their hands, that turned out to entail a baptism not only of moral aspiration but also of art, philosophy, economics, the interpretation of the historical process and the human situation generally.

Finally, in Chapter 5, I explained the concept of 'integral evangelisation' – the aim of which is the metaphorical baptism of the culture as well as the literal baptism of the individuals who inhabit it. I sought to lay out some of the ways Catholic Christians can and should pursue it, using Friedrich von Hügel's distinction between 'intellectual', 'mystical' and 'institutional' aspects of the religious task when that task is conceived at its most profound and comprehensive. That last Chapter sought to draw together a number of the themes found in the rest of the book.

No doubt, those themes are too many. I realise there are, in fact, far too many ideas in this book for its own good. As at a Norwegian breakfast – the 'cold table' – the plethora of dishes, at least in the light of early morning, may repel. But – who knows? – things may turn out better. The variety of fare offered may also attract a like variety of diners.

I give a penultimate word to Anglicans, but an ultimate one to my own co-religionists – as in an 'unfashionable essay on the conversion of England' is only appropriate. In *Prospect for Christendom. Essays in Catholic Social Reconstruction*, Maurice Reckitt sought to express the benefits the realm can obtain from revelation in its synthesis with reason.

> [T]he consecrated intelligence of Christendom, in its thirst for Divine illumination, has been brought to the apprehension of a new outlook upon the meaning of life and the significance of human order. And whatever its historical limitations or contingent applications, the philosophy of Christendom does hand on to us bequests which we no more than any other age can afford to disregard or undervalue. The very notion of Christendom itself – a society acknowledging across all frontiers allegiance, as exhibited in its purposes and its values, to Christ the King; the validity of secular authority and the limits of that authority; the sacred rights, as against all such authority, of the person and the family; the acknowledgement of distributive justice; the relation of both authority and liberty to the

> functional principle; a measure of 'social asceticism' in the handling even of what are truly 'goods' – these are not principles of a purely historical interest or transient value. They are the elements in the foundation of any human order which under whatever forms, political or technological, deserves – or is likely – to endure.[219]

And Reckitt concludes, referring in his peroration to some of the great names of the Anglican 'clerisy':

> No human truth is secure from the corrosion of sentimentalism. Christendom, whether as ideal or as fact, is no exception. Yet the very word emphasizes the consoling truth that in struggling to approximate the life of our nation to the standards of a Christian realm we shall not be entering upon a totally unprecedented enterprise. This island was once a Christian society within a Christian civilization, explicitly accepting Christian goals for life, and regulative institutions directed to safeguarding the pursuit of such purposes. Not all the crimes and follies, the negligences and ignorances, of medieval man can destroy that fact … We have to think, to assess the proposals of others, and to act ourselves, as the heirs of a great tradition, alive in this land for a century through Coleridge and Maurice, Stewart Headlam and Scott Holland, Neville Figgis and Charles Gore.[220]

Shall we then echo the following words of another, more celebrated, member of Reckitt's group, T. S. Eliot, and say:

---

[219] M. B. Reckitt, 'Catholic Sociology and the English Situation', in idem. (ed), *Prospect for Christendom. Essays in Catholic Social Reconstruction* (London 1945), pp. 85-99, and here at p. 87.
[220] Ibid., p. 89.

> It is easier for the Church of England to become Catholic, than for the Church of Rome in England to become English … If England is ever to be in any appreciable degree converted to Christianity, it can only be through the Church of England.[221]

If as (Roman) Catholic Christians we do not altogether agree, it is because the potential of the Catholic Church in England cannot be naturalistically described – much less circumscribed. It has been said of Jones's *Anathemata*:

> Because at the Last Supper, on the cross, and in the Mass Jesus makes history of myth, he renews all this amassed tradition so that the cumulative maypole of human culture is no longer the barren 'mortised stake' of merely remembered or imagined form. Spiritually and therefore ontologically, it blooms. If this is always true within the Mass and especially at the moment of sacramental transformation, which is the poem's fictional context, it is also potentially true for the reader, for groups of people, and for our civilization.[222]

---

[221] T. S. Eliot, *Thoughts after Lambeth*, op. cit., p. 27.

[222] T. Dilworth, *The Shape of Meaning in the Poetry of David Jones*, op. cit., p. 255, with an internal citation of D. Jones, *The Anathemata* (London 1972), p. 190.